AT CLOSE QUARTERS

AT CLOSE QUARTERS

SOE CLOSE COMBAT PISTOL INSTRUCTOR COLONSEL HECTOR GRANT-TAYLOR

DAVID ARMSTRONG

FONTHILL

For Victoria, Emma and Jack, My Ka-Tet

Fonthill Media Limited
Fonthill Media LLC
www.fonthillmedia.com
office@fonthillmedia.com

First published 2013

A CIP catalogue record for this book is available from the British Library

Typeset in 10,5pt on 14pt Sabon LT
Typesetting by Fonthill Media
Printed in the UK

Connect with us
 facebook.com/fonthillmedia twitter.com/fonthillmedia

Contents

By The Rt. Hon. Viscount Slim

In 1945, just after the bomb was dropped on Hiroshima and World War Two ended in South East Asia, I was ordered to report as ADC to Major-General D. T. Cowan of Burma fame. The general was now Commander of the British and Indian Forces who were about to occupy our designated territory in Japan. The division was being made ready at Nasik, India before shortly sailing from Bombay to Kure, Japan.

It was decided that the general should have a trained bodyguard as it was uncertain how the Japanese would react and behave under occupation. Together with four selected Gurkhas and the general's driver we reported to a Lieutenant-Colonel Grant-Taylor for a two-week close quarter battle (CQB) course.

I had never heard of or met Grant-Taylor. It became quickly apparent that he was a tough, unusual, highly motivated instructor and master of some unique skills and techniques—shooting to kill with handgun and Tommy gun.

Grant-Taylor was a natural and seasoned teacher. He taught with persistence and encouragement, and with some added humour. He was a hard taskmaster who demanded total concentration with constant rehearsal and practise. Grant-Taylor and I worked late into the night with blackboard and chalk, developing various bodyguard scenarios, which we rehearsed at length the next day. At the end of a fortnight we felt reasonably competent.

Many years later whilst serving with the Special Air Service (SAS) I saw an opportunity to introduce CQB into our operational training.

By then, of course, the world had moved swiftly on and, though a few fundamentals remained, Grant-Taylor's systems and techniques were out of date.

Close Quarter Battle required modernising and adapting to the now available new technology and equipment. We put together a small expert team to enhance CQB and its side issues, for present and future SAS operational requirements. It was successfully achieved. Furthermore we had immediate technical support from the Ministry of Defence in the building of our indoor and outdoor range facilities utilising electronics and modern training aids. I think the likeable Grant-Taylor would have been the first to admire our efforts.

I agreed to write this foreword because I believe that Fairbairn, Sykes and Grant-Taylor, together with those they taught as instructors, have not had from World War Two, the deserved recognition for their CQB skills and techniques, particularly given to special forces, Commandos and those that fought behind the lines. Many owe them much for their preparation for battle.

I have also been impressed by the author's historical investigation and research of CQB in World War Two and wish his book every success. It is after all, a small part of military history.

John Slim
House of Lords
March 2013

Colonel Grant-Taylor: Mystery Man

I first came upon the name of Colonel Grant-Taylor many years ago whilst undergoing some informal pistol training at the hands of a former airborne forces trooper. Within the modern close quarter combatives and special operations research community much is known about Second World War silent killing instructors such as W. E. Fairbairn, Bill Sykes and Rex Applegate. However regarding the mysterious Grant-Taylor there was very little.

At that point I had a basic knowledge of point shooting and was aware of 'instinctive' shooting methods as used by special forces, although I had never had the opportunity to train in these skills.

That was about to change.

'I'm going to show you the Grant-Taylor way of shooting,' my instructor rumbled. He then proceeded to lay out the techniques that he had been taught during the war.

'You hold the weapon close to your body, out in front. Keep your wrists tight and squeeze the whole gun, not just the trigger. Clench your hand! Keep your legs bent at the knee, and squat down to make yourself a smaller target!'

This was followed by, 'Now let the target have it—double tap him! Bang, Bang!' Twenty minutes later after some fine-tuning, I was getting consistent shots on target, and I could see how it would be a viable and easy-to-learn shooting method for soldiers clearing a trench or closing down an enemy.

Throughout my career in the teaching of close quarter combat, especially those related to close range firearms work, I was fortunate enough to have been shown the Grant-Taylor method by two remarkable individuals that had studied under the man himself.

The first was one of my original firearms instructors who had used it to good effect at the front-line of military operations during the Second World War. He was the person who first introduced me to the world of Second World War based combatives and more specifically, the instinctive shooting method that he learned during his wartime service. He was the real deal, a prolific firearms exponent and boxer all his life—the spirit of good health and the bulldog determination that epitomises that generation. An Airborne Forces trooper for most of the war, he'd 'gone in' by glider on D-day, only to have it veer off course and have to fight his way back to his main party of comrades. He also saw action in Palestine and in the China-Burma-India theatre of operations. He was a genuine tough guy. When I began training in and researching close quarter combat and pistol shooting, it was he who gave me the heads up about what worked and what didn't, and from him I learned the mechanics of the Grant-Taylor techniques, such as stance, firing and aggressive mindset. My interest was piqued. Now that I understood the method of Grant-Taylor's shooting style, I realised I needed to know how he came to these conclusions. I knew plenty about what he could do, but little about the man himself. He was a cipher.

The other was a former Commanding Officer of the SAS, Colonel John Slim, the 2nd Viscount Slim, who also showed me the handgun techniques, but more importantly instructed me in the context of close quarter pistol shooting for room combat.

One of my most informative (and surreal) training moments was being shown the intricacies of Grant-Taylor's room combat method in Viscount Slim's office in the House of Lords by Viscount Slim himself. This aristocratic octogenarian calmly entered the room with his finger pointed in a mock pistol style, giving a very erudite commentary about how to eliminate a series of bad guys at close range, all the while firing out imaginary double taps.

So who the hell was this Grant-Taylor?

From this start point there began a long and investigative journey that consisted of five-years' worth of research and detective work. It was littered with many pitfalls, red herrings and disinformation.

The journey had taken me (both literally and figuratively) from the corridors of power in Westminster, to the winter Highlands of Scotland, the burning heats of the Middle East and Israel, to the sultry and dangerous locations of Taliban controlled Pakistan and to the anti-terrorist training units and CQB facilities of the UK. Each would provide a small clue about Grant-Taylor that I was sure would all fit together to make up a bigger picture. It was a disassembled jigsaw looking for completion.

However before you can begin any investigation, the wise investigator should acquaint themselves with any relevant information that is already out there. In the case of the Grant-Taylor investigation, it seemed it was prudent to discover what had already been discovered about the man.

So where to begin? Well if you were to read the SOE personnel file in the National Archives or the current spate of online biographies and tales relating to one Leonard Hector Grant-Taylor, you could be forgiven for concluding that the man in question was a product of the English old-boy network, a scion of the upper classes, privately educated and with private means, that enabled him to travel and adventure across the globe in the inter-war years (1918-1939).

The current biographies state that Leonard Duncan Hector Grant-Taylor, who, according to his Second World War personnel files, was born on 25 September 1891 in the district of Banffshire in Scotland. His father is named as John Grant-Taylor, a director of a registered insurance company who regularly travelled between Scotland, London and the USA.

The young Leonard's love affair with the art of the marksman is said to have started in the late 1890s. It is alleged that his father took him to see that showman and legend of the old west, Buffalo Bill Cody, and his Wild West Show, when the troupe paid one of their visits to England to perform for the masses.

To a young boy from the lowlands of Scotland the sight of real-life cowboys and expert marksmen performing trick-shots, with both rifle and pistol, and with a legacy of such names as Annie Oakley, Wild Bill Hicock and Texas Jack must have been a sight to behold as these legends of the old west performed. The shows also demonstrated bronco riding, roping, and other skills that would later become part of public rodeos. From that moment on the art of the gun would become his overriding passion and it would not be very long before Hector would be living out a dream come true and seeing what was left of the Wild West, first hand.

Due to their family and business ties with America, the Grant-Taylor family often made trips to Boston to visit the young Leonard's paternal grandfather, who had immigrated to the United States and built a prosperous life for himself. These visits to the USA would also have been a chance to look over new investments and business opportunities, certainly during one trip to Montana, the young Leonard met a Montana cattleman by the name of Charles Tracy.

In an interview given many years later, Grant-Taylor awarded this man the recognition of teaching him how to handle a pistol. The man, Tracy, would have taught the young Leonard the practicalities of pistol and rifle shooting that would have been necessary in his everyday trade as a rancher and cattleman.

The Grant-Taylor family, it was said, lived an affluent lifestyle and as successful business people they were what the upper-class would have called 'new money'. By the end of his first decade the young Leonard was educated at a private school in Yorkshire (Mount St Mary's) and showed a flair for literature and the written word. His efforts would later take him on to academic success at Cambridge, where he would receive a BA in Modern History and English Literature.

A veteran of the First World War, his previous military experience had included four years as a regimental adjutant soldering around India, Bengal and the north-west frontier and during his service in France it was stated that he had received the Croix de Guerre.

After the First World War, he gained employment at the Home Office on two separate occasions, the first between the years of 1925-1927 and later between 1929-1931 when he gave his occupation as 'schoolteacher/lecturer'. During this period he is said to have taught the British Police Special Branch the close-range shooting method which he spent his life refining, and many have stated that his work for the Home Office was a cover for espionage work.

During the 1920s and 1930s he is also supposed to have travelled to the furthest corners of the empire and seems to have been an extremely well travelled man having visited Holland, France, Germany, Egypt, India and Italy, and having both French and Urdu as language skills.

This was followed by tales of his working undercover in the organised crime families of Chicago, learning the skills of assassination from mob hit-men, to training the Federal Bureau of Investigation in pistol shooting, running resistance operations in China, to even being one of the police officers (seconded) that shot down John Dillinger outside the Biograph Theatre in Chicago in 1934.

He is said to have been married only once to a woman by the initials of W. E. L. S. Rix, and they lived happily at their home in Surrey until the outbreak of hostilities in 1939, when Grant-Taylor received a wartime commission before being quickly recruited for the fledgling commando operations and later Special Operations Executive (SOE).

Legend has it that his most famous commando exploits were during the early part of the war, running hit and run commando raids into occupied Europe during 1940-1. During the first he is said to have led a team to assassinate a group of Norwegian Quislings gathered at a local bar. A following operation to eliminate a group of Luftwaffe aces in France also involved Grant-Taylor and his team storming the building and shooting them down.

During this period, Grant-Taylor was injured and taken off the active service list and transferred to SOE as an instructor. He also later claimed that he had at one time been recruited by the British Secret Service to bump off a German agent operating in Turkey that was sabotaging allied transportation of war goods. Grant-Taylor and his team allegedly isolated him, eliminated him with a knife and buried his body in nearby woods.

Following this, Grant-Taylor was operational, instructing in close quarter shooting in the Middle East, before being transferred to General William Slim's 14th Army in Burma to do more of the same.

For many years there was a rumour that he was said to have perished in a plane crash off the straits of Malacca in the Indian Ocean, and that postwar he had indeed survived the war and stood as a conservative member of parliament back home in Great Britain. Following this he supposedly disappeared and his whereabouts remain a mystery to this day.

All of the above, or at least 95%, is pure fabrication, misinformation and complete falsehood.

This information has thrown many a good researcher and historian (and a few bad ones) down a very precarious track filled with false information and blind alleys, which quite often leads them to make rather exotic leaps of faith with the truth. Many have portrayed Grant-

Taylor as a ruthless cold blooded hit man (or an even more cloak and dagger disposal man) with a chiselled jaw-line and steely ice-cold killer stare. One wag even suggested that he was known internationally as the 'King of Assassins'.

This is complete nonsense and completely unfair to a dedicated professional soldier.

It is the aim of this work and its author to set the record straight once and for all regarding the life of Colonel Grant-Taylor and to highlight his teaching in the art of close quarter battle which is still in use today by the world's elite counter-terrorist forces. Much of the material that is contained within this book has never before been revealed to the public, and will no doubt cast a very different light upon the man that military historians thought they knew.

And while his story is in no way a cloak and dagger spy story as has previously been touted by other writers, it is still a remarkable tale of deception, skulduggery, lies, betrayal, and ultimately redemption.

And so, dear reader, may I introduce to you to the truth that is behind the cipher, the enigma, the mysterious man known as Colonel Hector Grant-Taylor.

David Armstrong
July 2012

CHAPTER ONE:

The Road to War

1914-1920

When you're wounded and left on Afghanistan's plains,
And the women come out to cut up what remains,
Jest roll to your rifle and blow out your brains
An' go to your Gawd like a soldier.
Go, go, go like a soldier,
Go, go, go like a soldier,
Go, go, go like a soldier,
So-oldier ~of~ the Queen!

Rudyard Kipling

The man that would later become known as Leonard Hector Duncan Grant-Taylor was in fact born to much more modest surroundings and to less impressive titles than he would later claim.

He was in fact born plain Leonard Taylor on 25 September 1889 in the district of Newton, in the northern city of Manchester. His parents were John Henry Taylor, a travelling salesman and would be local business entrepreneur and Jane Taylor (née Hart) a housewife. The couple had married in Chorlton, Lancashire in 1883. His paternal ancestors originally hailed from Ireland, with his Grandfather moving his family over to the British mainland in the early 1850s to seek work on the railways as a labourer.

The Taylors lived at 64 Woodward Street, a respectable working class area, where in the early 1890s John set up a store as a grocer, supplying the local neighbourhood. His widowed mother, Ann, also lived with the family, working part time in the shop and part time assisting with the new baby, Leonard.

The family greengrocery business apparently thrived, thus enabling the Taylors to have the means to set themselves up in relative comfort. In January 1895, a second son, Cyril was born. The family at this time needed, and could modestly afford, a larger property and so moved to the more well-to-do area of Miles Platting.

By the time of the early 1900s John had taken on a further role as an insurance officer. This is a grand title for what in reality was the local insurance man in the area—collecting tallies for death and house insurance, knocking door to door and coming to collect the money at the end of the working week.

John continued in this trade for at least the next two decades up until his retirement in 1917. Leonard by contrast seems to have been an academic at school and keen on the literature of the time. Tales of Victorian adventurers and explorers, such as Rider Haggard's *King Solomon's Mines* provided the boy with a taste for rip-roaring yarns and stories of life in the colonies of Africa, Asia and the Middle East.

It is fair to say that for a bright, young man of his time, it was easy for the young Leonard to want to aspire to be the very epitome of the English gentleman of a certain caste—unpretentious, stiff upper-lip, athletic, and someone who believes in fair play. These people are generally seen as self reliant (a quality instilled into them in the public school system), and ready to obey orders from their superiors. All in all they are good Christian gentleman.

Later claims in his wartime military files regarding his early education, appear to be completely unfounded. For example, according to his 1941 personnel file for SOE, he is supposed to have attended a private boarding school in Yorkshire (Mount St Mary's) and later graduated to Cambridge University where he received a BA.

Instead, it appears that this was a falsehood. In fact, he attended the local state education comprehensive school in Manchester, and never made it to the grandiose heights of upper class London universities.

What is fact, however, is that Leonard was a bright academic young man and it appears in his formative teenage years his teachers steered him towards the teaching profession and education system. The young Leonard seems to have had a natural talent for teaching—and this would be borne out also in his later years within the military system.

By the time he had left school he had acquired a job working as an uncertified day school teacher with the local borough council and he continued in this profession for several more years working quite happily.

In the spring of 1909, Jane Taylor, his mother, died. Mothers are so often the bond that glue the family together, and without whom there is the risk of the family losing their way and becoming fragmented. The men of the Taylor household were left alone.

For the Taylors, life would carry on in its routine way for the next five years. Meanwhile in the distant horizon of mainland Europe, the drums of war were gaining momentum.

It was a bright spring morning when the small, stocky but well presented young gentlemen entered the local recruitment office for His Majesty's armed forces. The queue for enrolment literally stretched around the block with all manner of young men, from working class tradesmen and apprentices to white collar workers, each willing to sign up and accept the King's coin. For honour, for duty, for patriotism. For King and Country.

Over recent months, with the war gathering more fervour a wave of young men volunteered for military service. The easiest way was to go round to your local recruiting station, assure the recruiting sergeant there that you were over the minimum age of nineteen, and you literally signed your papers. There was such enthusiasm at the start of the war that queues were the norm. At first, they would have rallies, or appeals at football matches, and there would just be a series of tables set out and you would queue up and sign on there and then.

Leonard Taylor began his army career by joining The Black Watch (Royal Highlanders), where after completing basic training at Aldershot in July 1914 he was posted to front-line service in France for ten months, in which he and his platoon were based at Richebourg St Vaast. It was during this period that he saw service at Artois and was wounded in action at the battle of Neuve Chappelle. The battle was a British based offensive that began on 10 March 1915 in the Artois region. The British however (due to a lack of artillery shells it was later claimed) were unable to exploit the advantage. The ultimate aim of the battle was to cause a rupture in the German lines which would then be exploited with a rush on the Aubers Ridge and possibly even Lille, which at that time, was a major enemy communications centre. Three hundred men of the Royal West Kents, commanded by a lieutenant and a 2nd lieutenant, emerged—the battalion had suffered a total of 450 casualties. Somewhere in the midst of this conflict, Leonard Taylor sustained a wartime injury and was repatriated.

After convalescence he was transferred to the 5th (Reserve Battalion) the Queen's Own Royal West Kent Regiment, (QORWK) where he received a commission in November 1915 as a 2nd Lieutenant. The 4th Battalion of the QORWK had been formed in 1915 when it became named the 4th Reserve Battalion. A year later it had absorbed the 5th Reserve Battalion into its ranks and had moved to its wartime home of Tunbridge Wells

As for Taylor's commission, whilst it was not uncommon for a soldier from the ranks to be promoted to an officer rank, a large percentage did tend to come from families with military connections or the gentry, with a public school education being essential. As an example in 1913, about two per cent of regular officers had been promoted from the ranks. The officer corps, during the war, consisted of regular officers from the peacetime army, officers who had been granted permanent commissions during the war, officers who had been granted temporary commissions for the duration of the war, territorial army officers commissioned during peacetime, officers commissioned from the ranks of the pre-war regular and territorial army and temporary officers commissioned from the ranks for the duration of the war alone.

In 1915, it was discovered that 12,290 men serving in the ranks had been members of a university or public school Officers' Training Corps (OTC). Most applied for (and were granted) commissions, while others who did not apply, were also commissioned. The military, in desperate times, needed bright young and resourceful men and they were not concerned about what social standing they came from, only that they could become good officers and inspirational leaders of men. Direct commissioning largely ceased early in 1916. From then on, most new officers had served in the ranks first. Taylor was one of the latter breed.

For much of 1915–1916 he went through a variety of training courses geared to bring a young officer up to speed with the latest tactics and methods for fighting a modern war and being able to lead and train a body of soldiers. This included machine gun training at the Number 14 Officer Training Battalion (OTB) range in Berkhamsted, the standard army musketry course at the Army School of Musketry, Hythe, Kent, and Officers' Equestrian Training at Forest Row, East Grinstead. He also attended a course of physical instruction training, bayonet fighting, as well as the Brigade of Guards school of Instruction. By May 1916, he had received a further promotion to the rank of 2nd Lieutenant (Acting Captain) with the QORWK.

Throughout 1917 he attended further officer's training programmes such as lessons in topography, map reading and field sketching under Lieutenant Courtney Terrell, a noted map-reader and field craft expert, at the Inns of Court Officer Training Centre in Chelsea (IOCTC). The IOCTC was responsible for training literally thousands of British officers prior to their deployment to the front-line.

This was further supplemented by attending a senior officer's bombing course in Surrey and a camouflage course in Hyde Park, London. As an acting captain, he was also involved in the training of platoons and divisions for offensive action at Aux-le-Château, a small farming town north-west of Arras in France.

Aux-le-Château was one of the main schools of instruction for the British Army during this period and its grounds included a mock-up trench system complete with demonstration troops, small arms ranges and was used for delivering instructional and refresher courses in tactics to officers and Senior NCOs. One of the local large houses was requisitioned as a Headquarters with satellite hutments added as required for stores and accommodation.

This was not unusual as many training schools and facilities were developed behind the lines in France and Flanders and the other theatres of war. Specialist courses on tactics and new equipment development such as the machine gun and poison gas were developed, and officers were regularly withdrawn in order to attend. Not only did they update the officer on new techniques but they also provided a welcome respite from the strain of front line command.

Later on that year, and perhaps of special interest given his later work during the war, was Taylor's attainment of his Marksman's Instructor's Certificate. At the time, this was the standard training in personal sidearms and took place at one of the army's many revolver schools at Wareham, Dorset. The purpose of this type of training was to give the officer or NCO the basic knowledge and to be able to prove competency for small arms shooting, usually working with the .445

Webley Revolver.

All this training was to stand him in good stead as he had recently been appointed the Commandant of the Army School of Instruction, based in Tunbridge Wells, Kent. The military command, in the form of his senior officer General M. G Wilkinson, recognising that they had a forward-thinking young officer, capable of running an exceptional series of training programmes decided that Captain Taylor's skills were not to be wasted upon the battlefields, but rather doing what he did best—instructing.

The Tunbridge Wells School of Instruction was for officers and warrant officers and covered all the previous training that Captain Taylor had completed including field work, topography, military law and infantry bridge building. He also took a special interest in delivering the training personally at the senior officer's revolver course, working out on the ranges.

On the 11 November 1918, and with the war in Europe coming to an end, the 4th QORWK arrived in Quetta, India, where it was to play a part in another conflict: Afghanistan.

There is a long history of British military operations in Afghanistan, and romantic notions of the great game aside, it was a dirty and bloody series of conflicts over a series of three successive wars between 1839 and 1919.

The main reason was because of the location of a strategic mountain range, the Hindu Kush, which provided access for the British between Russia and India. The British needed control of the route and were prepared to do everything in their power to achieve that aim, at first by diplomatic means, but later through the strength of its military might.

A series of diplomatic and armed skirmishes followed over the next eighty years, until in 1919 a peace treaty was broken by Amir Amanullah Khan, who subsequently declared independence from British control and proclaimed a jihad, or Holy War. His plan was to encourage a popular revolt on the north west frontier with the hope of seizing the old Afghan provinces west of the River Indus that had been captured by the Sikhs many years before.

Amanullah believed that the British would be too war-weary to resist after the onslaught of the war in Europe and he sent a detachment of Afghan troops across the border into India to occupy the town of Bagh. He was wrong. The British response was nothing if not expected and they threw the might of the military machine at the provocation. The

Third Afghan War had begun.

At the time of his arrival in India, Captain Leonard Taylor was the adjutant, acting as an assistant to the commanding officer. His duties would have included organization, administration, and discipline, and within the regiment he would have held a vital and important position.

The QORWK had only been in country for less than three weeks when they took part in the assault on the Afghan fortress of Spin Baldak. Spin Baldak was a remote border town in the Khandahar province of Afghanistan, and its strategically placed Fort and satellite buildings stood proud on top of one of the many mountain peaks in the region.

The British assault, under the command of General Richard Wapshore, began at dawn when several cavalry units and small group with machine-guns made a detour to get behind Spin Boldak to cut its communication with Kandahar. After a six-hour artillery bombardment, the assault was successful and the fort was seized and occupied. Of about 600 Afghan soldiers holding it, 186 were killed and 176 taken prisoner. The assault left four British soldiers killed, and one officer and other ranks wounded in action.

Wapshare left three infantry units at Spin Boldak and withdrew the reminder of his force to New Chaman, and while the capture of the fort was a tactical victory for the British, the enemy's subsequent threat of counter attack caused the British to tie up much needed military resources in the south when they could have been better used elsewhere.

Whatever his exact role was in the taking of the Fort at Spin Baldak, Captain Taylor received several Mentions In Despatches during his time in India and Afghanistan, most notably from General Sir Charles Munro the Commander-in-Chief of Indian Operations, General Sir Richard Wapshore the Commander of the 4th Quetta Division, General Gordon the Commander of 44th Brigade and General Hardy the Commander of the Southern Column. As well as his British War Medal for his service during the First World War, he also received the India General Service Medal with the George V clasp for service during 1919.

With his time in India almost at an end, Captain Taylor seems to have been searching for a role that kept him in the region and asked for a transfer to one of the Indian Army regiments, with his preferences seeming to be the 36th Sikh Regiment or the 102nd Grenadiers. This was a reasonable career move for a young officer that had a wealth of operational experience in several different theatres of operations, as well as his linguistic skills and knowledge of the region.

However after sitting a stringent medical exam he was rejected by the medical board and remained with the QORWK. The regiment finished active operations five months later and arrived back at Plymouth on 21 November 1919. Less than two months later he had completed his four years' service and decided to leave the military. The reasons remain unclear, but the most likely theories are because of refusal by the Indian regiments, or that he wished to try his hand at the world of commerce in civilian life.

By the time that his military service was due to end, it appears that Captain Leonard Taylor was already looking ahead, hoping to cast off the reality of his working class roots, and was well under way to developing a new, imagined persona, that he hoped would raise him up to become a part of the upper class military establishment. As is standard for an army officer leaving the service, he was required to submit to a questionnaire giving his personal and background details. This form was then kept on file in case the officer was called back as a reservist or should he wish to revive his military career. Captain Leonard Taylor officially left the British Army on 23 February 1920.

Taylor wasted no time in setting out his stall, no matter how false. Of his personal background he claimed that he had been born in London and had attended a London University. As we know this was not the case, but what was even more telling was on his next of kin form where he claimed that his mother (as his next of kin) was one J. Taylor-Marsh of Speldhurst, Kent, who had remarried following the death of his father, John, and had moved south to live with Leonard Taylor's wealthy step-father, also called John.

Once again, as we are now aware, this was a complete fabrication. The J. Taylor-Marsh in question was in fact a Mrs Jessie Lorraine Taylor Marsh, born in 1870 and was the wife of a successful engineer and inventor John Taylor Marsh of Kent. Where Leonard Taylor came across the name of this innocent couple is not known, although the Taylor Marsh's did have a nephew that served during the First World War and Mrs Marsh herself had worked as a volunteer nurse in Kent, tending to injured service personnel back from the war. So it is not inconceivable that Leonard Taylor at some point came across their name by chance and worked it in to the bogus background story that he had invented for himself. This is possibly the ultimate shedding of his family and working class roots, by disowning his parents, in favour of strangers who fitted in to the fictitious persona that he had created.

Despite the postwar patriotic flag waving and promises of 'jobs for heroes', the economic reality of the depression era was that employment and the opportunities for business at that time were extremely limited. Indeed many veterans felt nothing but contempt for the establishment and political leaders that had sent them off to be slaughtered in a foreign field. And the burning question that haunted many veterans was, what did we risk our lives for? Was the cost of the lives worth it?

Jobs for heroes appears to have been nothing more than a slogan as many men were side-tracked, either through disability, being shell-shocked or just plain old lack of opportunity. For officers, it was just as tough. Having served in a good regiment was no guarantee of opening doors to the world of the city or business. Having the right background, however, was even more imperative in civilian life for an ex-army officer, especially one who claimed to be privately educated, of wealthy independent means, and one who had had a 'good and interesting war'.

And while Leonard Taylor had obviously served his country well during his military career, transferring those skills over to civilian life was going to be difficult. So he did what any forthright and keen to get on young man would do in difficult economic times—he told the establishment what they wanted to hear and massaged the truth about his origins. You want a privately educated university graduate? I'll give you one. You want someone of independent means that has travelled and comes from an upper class background? No problem, I can do that. You want a chap from a titled Scottish family? I'm your man.

But that is the problem with lies, they breed and develop and grow, quite often spiralling out of control, until the person that tells them is no longer the person they once were and they end up becoming consumed by their own deceptions.

CHAPTER TWO

The Many Wives
of Mr Grant-Taylor

1920-1939

A man who has two women loses his soul. But a man who has two houses loses his head.

Proverb—Anon

The 1920s seem to have been a cataclysmic time for Leonard Taylor. He had left behind a successful career in the British Army in 1920 and the period between 1920 and 1925 are the most undocumented of his life. Great swathes of his time are unaccounted for within those five years, and there is precious little information about how he earned his living or of his personal life. This part of his story may never truly be known.

What is known is that sometime during that half decade a new man was created—not born, but created. He was a cipher, a ghost that did not really exist. He was pieced together bit by bit like Frankenstein's monster, a name here, a back-story there, over a period of years. He was Leonard Taylor, but with a splash of glamour and gravitas. Where did the inspiration for the 'Hector' and the 'Duncan' and the 'Grant' come from being? They were certainly popular names of the time and many have speculated or tried to link them in some way to his supposed Scottish heritage.

Of course as we now know there was no Scottish heritage or connection to Leonard Taylor. It may simply be that he was looking for a certain level of aristocracy in his name, so as to fit in with his new biography. There is a train of thought that states that when a man changes his identity, he cannot resist the temptation to keep one minor

24

detail for old time's sake. This was certainly true in the case of Leonard Taylor.

All that we know is that it was during this period that his self-made legend started to take shape. In espionage terms a legend is a fictitious persona created for the intelligence officer, and which is geared towards achieving a certain aim whether it is access to secrets or by secreting the person into a position of authority to influence or to spread disinformation.

The man had changed his name to a grand double-barrelled title, he had moved south away from his native north-west thus severing any remaining family links completely, and began falsifying the factual details of his parents as well as his date and place of birth (once again claiming that he hailed from a titled family who lived in Ballindaloch, Banffshire, Scotland).

There is, however, strong evidence that he yearned to return to his pre-war profession of teaching, but having been away on military service any qualifications that he had previously acquired would have been obsolete. Not that this was a restriction to finding employment as a teacher. In the 1920s and '30s the necessary background and qualification checks of today were not in evidence. Vetting of staff was incredibly vague and a little woolly, with positions being filled by a friend-of-a-friend or upon recommendation of a colleague rather than through an interview process. Teacher's wages of the day, whilst acceptable, were still comparatively poorly paid and few had any qualifications from a university. There were many examples of exceptionally competent teachers during this period, whether or not they had formal qualifications is another matter.

However, it seems that despite his having respectable employment in a variety of teaching positions, Leonard Taylor was restricted from rising socially—or at least in his eyes. He was essentially a lower middle class chap that aspired to higher things and was curtailed by his lack of connections.

Unfortunately, there were obviously doors closed to him that no amount of money could open, and instead were only applicable to those within the old boy network. In short he could not climb to where he desired to be on the many rungs of the class structure ladder. And as we have previously seen, he did what many individuals in this class-restrictive environment did. He re-invented himself.

Stated details of this period are vague, but what we know for sure is that the first official sighting of the man that later became known as Leonard Hector Grant-Taylor occurred on 3 April 1926, when he married a Minnie Louise Abbot at a ceremony in Kentish Town, London. Minnie Abbot was the daughter of William and Frances Abbot, owners of a factory that made piano frames. She was raised in a respectable middle class home and after leaving school had desires to become a school teacher. She later attended Norwich University in order to attain her degree and she subsequently went on to devote herself to her career teaching in the London area.

Minnie was a down to earth person with a strong cockney accent and no pretensions. She was a constant figure in the lives of her young nieces and nephews and loved her family very much.

So it came as a complete surprise when, in her late thirties, she met the much younger Grant-Taylor, and after a brief courtship they married. Minnie had already been bridesmaid to both her younger sisters and the family felt that she was a bit too keen to be married when the first opportunity arose.

According to Minnie's family, Hector was very handsome and knew how to charm a lady, and it was due to this devastating combination that Minnie fell head over heels in love with him, becoming completely besotted. The only information that they knew about him was his name and that he worked as a schoolmaster.

So who was this ladykiller? Where did he come from? What was his background? The Abbott family never got to the bottom of that. Hector never spoke about his family and was reticent to talk about his background. The only family reference is when he names his father on his marriage certificate as John Grant-Taylor (deceased)—insurance director.

The couple moved into an address at Forty Lane, Wembley and settled into the normalcy of middle class suburban life. Later, at Grant-Taylor's insistence the couple moved to the exclusive Parliament Hills Mansions, Lissenden Gardens, in London. Hector, was at that time working at a school in the London Borough area, and would supplement his income in his spare time by lecturing in the subjects of Egyptology and economic history to inmates at both Pentonville and Parkhurst prisons. He was also still in touch with his military roots, and in 1926 was a volunteer instructor with the rank of Acting Major for Colonel Sir Philip Carlebach's territorial force, the 1st City of London Cadet Brigade of the Royal Fusiliers.

Based at a training depot in London, Grant-Taylor was one of several Instructors with experience gained during the First World War that would put the part-time troops through a series of structured military disciplines. This included an instructional tour of France with the Brigade as guests of the French military. However, closer to home and scratching beneath the surface of the marriage, it appears all was not been well.

The Abbott family felt that Grant-Taylor was taking advantage of Minnie in numerous ways, primarily by spending large portions of her money as well as disappearing for weekends without explaining where he had been. Obviously this type of behaviour would cause any number of rows between the couple, but despite all this Minnie would always back down, for the simple reason that she loved Leonard Grant-Taylor completely. Things soon came to a head in September 1930, when after four years of marriage, Minnie walked out on him and returned to the Abbott family home. She discovered that he had been fleecing their bank account and had got himself into a number of growing debts—which he obviously was having trouble re-paying. One of these debts was a lease on an apartment in the elite Upper Berkeley Square, Mayfair area of London. Then a month later came the news that blew Minnie's world apart—Hector Grant-Taylor had married again.

How his bigamy had been discovered is not documented, but it would not be inconceivable for him to have been spotted carousing around London with a young lady on his arm by Minnie's family and friends. And of course there is that most secretive of secret information networks, the teacher's grapevine.

The lady in question was twenty-six-year-old Eleanor Ann Thomas with whom Grant-Taylor had been having an affair, and had become infatuated. The couple had met at the school in Paddington where both Grant-Taylor and Eleanor Thomas worked as schoolteachers. After a passionate whirlwind romance, which culminated with Grant-Taylor proposing, the couple married at a ceremony in London on 30 September 1930. The marriage certificate gives us several tantalising clues as to the extent of Grant-Taylor's deceptions at this time.

For instance, in his marriage to Minnie Abbott he gave himself the name Leonard Duncan Hector Grant-Taylor, but in his bigamous marriage he reverses the middle names and titles making himself Leonard Hector Duncan Grant-Taylor, in the hope of confusing anyone who may conduct a cursory check. He interestingly gives his profession as 'soldier' rather than schoolmaster, and names his father as Hector Duncan Grant-Taylor with his profession also as a soldier.

Clearly Grant-Taylor was living a lie, and passing these fabrications on to a possibly naïve and impressionable young woman whose head had been turned by tales of adventuring in distant lands, and by being wined and dined by an older man who seemed to be living an affluent lifestyle. All that was about to stop. The couple honeymooned at the swanky Queens Hotel, Hastings, for a fortnight before returning home to Grant-Taylor's apartment in London, where he was promptly arrested and detained by the police. The scandal finally broke and was eventually played out across the tabloid newspapers.

Minnie was obviously shell-shocked by Grant-Taylor's actions, but had to go through the indignity of attending his court hearing prior to his sentencing where she came face to face with the other woman, Eleanor Thomas. The two women met, shook hands politely, and tried to work through the mess they had become embroiled in. Minnie later commented that the two of them had got on rather well considering the circumstances.

On 11 November 1930, Leonard Duncan Hector Grant-Taylor was sentenced at the Old Bailey by Judge Sir Ernest Wild to seventeen months imprisonment for bigamy. He was to serve his time at H.M.P. Wormwood Scrubs. Human nature being what it is, the salacious details were served up in the tabloids of the day. The *Daily Mirror* on 12 November 1930 ran with the headline, 'Lectured in Prison: Now in gaol himself—schoolmaster sentenced for bigamy.'

The Abbott family distanced Minnie and themselves from the whole sordid mess and set about closing ranks, trying to rebuild their lives. Minnie filed for divorce from Grant-Taylor in March 1931 citing the grounds of desertion and adultery with Eleanor Ann Thomas. She subsequently received her Decree Absolute on 30 May 1932.

After this devastating period of her life, Minnie carried on working in her teaching career until she reached retirement age. She kept the Taylor name (though dropped the 'Grant' from the title) then moved down to Folkstone, Kent and devoted herself to her family and friends.

The Abbott family in later years leaked a story to distant family and neighbours, in the hope of mollifying and killing the story dead, that Hector Grant-Taylor had died in a bombing raid during the Blitz of 1940. Minnie Taylor died in 1978 at the age of 92.

So how did Grant-Taylor go from being a respected former army officer, schoolmaster, husband and pillar of the local community to a prisoner at His Majesty's pleasure? How did he fall so far and so fast? His liberty was removed, his wives had left him, and his reputation was in tatters. We will of course never know for sure and can only speculate upon the reasons for his financial shenanigans as well as his extra-marital affair and bigamy. Of his financial misgivings and affair one could argue that he had seen an opportunity in the moderately wealthy Minnie Abbott, and was keen to take advantage of the finer things of life (at her expense) and of living a lifestyle that provided him with the best of both worlds. A respectable and financially comfortable well-off wife at home, and on the other hand a lifestyle of drinking clubs, nightlife and good looking younger women. He wanted to have his cake and also to devour it.

It is perhaps his reasons for committing bigamy that are the most mysterious. Many modern day psychologists believe that there are only a limited number of reasons behind a person taking such an action. Sheer laziness is usually the most prevalent, as most will agree that it is far easier to get married than un-married, and even more so in the 1920s and '30s when divorce proceedings were the preserve of the rich and influential. Even this was no guarantee of a swift divorce.

Another possible reason is that the bigamy is sexually motivated. An older man is besotted with a younger attractive woman and he reasons that it would take marriage and financial security to be able to keep her. This certainly bears many similarities to Grant-Taylor's modus operandi. Whatever the reasoning, both women were in the path of the steam-train that was Hector Grant-Taylor and both, in their own ways, paid the price. As for Grant-Taylor he truly reaped what he had sowed.

Wormwood Scrubs Prison is located in the area of inner West London. Known as The Scrubs, the prison was constructed entirely from convict labour and the design was based on the infamous Sing Sing prison in New York. By the summer of 1875 enough bricks had been prepared to build the prison's first block, whose ground floor was finished as winter began. Construction was finally completed in 1891.

In any prisoner's life there is always 'before the fall', when they endeavour to get away with their crime and remain at liberty, and then there is *the* fall, which encompasses the arrest, trial, embarrassment and incarceration of the individual. For Grant-Taylor the fall was great and this must have been the lowest point of his life to date. He evidently kept on good behaviour while in prison as 'Prisoner number 7772 Grant-Taylor' was released three months early on 16 January, 1932, and set about the long road to re-building his life. After regaining his liberty he lodged with a Mr and Mrs Arthur and Helena Finch of Hillingdon West, initially to give himself a base from where he could begin again. The Finch's address was conveniently close to Uxbridge Cricket Club where Grant-Taylor, a lifelong cricket aficionado, would attend county games.

However his lodging arrangement seems to have been extended whilst he struggled to find employment, as not many schools would employ an ex-convict. Even while residing in Uxbridge he was not above reverting to his old tricks of deception, as he represented himself to the Finch's as a Lionel Hector Duncan Grant-Taylor. During this period Grant-Taylor avoided using his previous name, and was not conerned about falsifying details, in case it hampered his chances of a fresh start.

Things finally began to turn around for him in the spring of 1934 when he managed to secure employment as a teacher and instructor at one of the many unemployment social services centres that had sprung up over recent years. His role was to lecture on basic English and mathematics, and to provide physical training lessons.

In the 1920s, the British Government had set up a series of work camps for the unemployed in order to make them fit enough to work. They were termed 'Labour Instructional Centres' and the first opened in 1925. With the effect of the Great Depression in full swing, the number of camps inevitably increased so that by 1937 there were more than thirty training centres in operation.

Several of these centres were established in the Norfolk area, namely, at High Lodge, West Tofts, and Cranwich Heath. The new Norfolk sites were all on land leased from the Forestry Commission. Five further training centres were also established at Bourne in Lincolnshire, Fermyn Woods near Brigstock in Northamptonshire, Presteign in Radnorshire, Swanton Novers near Melton Constable in Norfolk, and Shobdon in Herefordshire.

The camps had an almost quasi-military to feel to them, with an average of twenty men sharing a hut. The men were up at 6.30 a.m. and then were marched to their jobs from the parade ground in the military style. After a full day of work, which could include anything from physical training to basic reading and writing of the English language, to digging in the fields, or breaking rocks in the quarry, the men were marched back to their quarters and at 10.30 p.m. the night watchman would call the roll, army-style. Many of the Instructors—like Grant-Taylor—were either retired teachers or former soldiers capable of instilling discipline and a strong work ethic into their recruits.

It was during this period, working in the Norfolk region, that Grant-Taylor met, befriended, and courted, a young woman by the name of Wilhelmina Edna Laura Sophie Rix. Known as Sophie to her family and friends, at the time of her meeting Grant-Taylor she was only twenty-five years old, and lived and worked at the family owned pub, the Kings Arms Hotel in North Walsham, Norfolk. It did not take long before Grant-Taylor once again used his not inconsiderable charms to woo his young lady friend with tales of overseas adventures, titled families and expensive treats and gifts. Using the deceiver's age old trick of a mixture of lies and truth combined, he represented himself as a former military officer that had successfully dabbled with commerce, but had trained as a schoolteacher.

His charms evidently worked on her, because a mere eight years after his first marriage, and four after his second bigamous marriage, Grant-Taylor proposed again. The couple were married at a Registry Office in the District of Smallburgh, Norfolk on 27 December 1934. Grant-Taylor was not being honest with his new wife; in fact he was downright manipulative and untruthful to her.

The marriage certificate, at least on Grant-Taylor's part, was a minefield of lies. Firstly, he named himself Hector Duncan Grant-Taylor (the Leonard had been completely dropped this time), and gave his age as forty (he was actually forty-five at this point); he gave his occupation as an instructor. Secondly he listed his residence as 31 Stanhope Gardens, Queen's Gate, London; and while this address in an exclusive part of West London was very real, there is no record of anyone by that name living there. More so because he was residing, albeit intermittently, with the Finches in Uxbridge, when he was not living on-site at the Labour Instructional Camps. Finally, of his family connections, he names his father as a Kenneth Bruce Grant-Taylor (deceased) a former lieutenant-colonel in the 4th Army.

Following the marriage, the newly married couple moved into a detached four-bedroom house in Richmond Park, London and by all accounts settled into a life of being happily married and of domestic bliss. By the late 1930s Hector Grant-Taylor had done many things to eradicate from his life the past of the man he used to be. He had changed his name multiple times, eradicated all trace of his northern accent and instead spoke with a 'plummy' home-counties drawl. He had adapted, chameleon-like, to his circumstances and social situation, and had more-or-less been constantly on the run from his numerous deceptions. He had become a hunted man, tortured by the failings of his own past. Therefore, just when he had given up all hope of becoming the aristocratic upper-class gentleman he truly aspired to be, and not the middle class chap that collected his wages on a Friday—and was chained to a quiet suburban lifestyle—a curious thing happened. It also gave him the chance of living out his dreams, and getting him back into the game that he so yearned for. After nearly twenty years of struggle, loss and deceptions, once again the wheel of fate turned and threw him back into where he had, in effect, started his career—with a war.

CHAPTER THREE

SOE: For Special Services 1940-42

There will be some who will be shocked by the methods advocated here.
To them I say 'In war you cannot afford the luxury of squeamishness.
Either you kill or capture, or you will be captured or killed. We've got
to be tough to win, and we've got to be ruthless—tougher and more
ruthless than our enemies.'

W. E. Fairbairn *Get-Tough*, 1942

One of the most revolutionary aspects of the Second World War was the advent of special operations and irregular warfare. The British seemingly had the monopoly on this during the first half of the last century thanks to their operational experience playing the 'great game' in Afghanistan and undercover warfare in Ireland. The rules of warfare were rapidly changing and the new prime minister, Winston Churchill, ever an—advocate of irregular operations, wanted the War Office to cater for this new strategy so as to throw its might against the German military machine.

The Special Operations Executive (SOE) was formed by the Minister of Economic Warfare, Hugh Dalton on 22 July 1940, to conduct espionage, assassination, and sabotage in occupied Europe as well as to assist and support local resistance movements. In Churchill's words he wanted a new organisation to 'set Europe ablaze'.

During its brief lifetime very few people were even aware of SOE's existence. By name it was usually referred to as 'Churchill's Secret Army' or the 'Ministry of Ungentlemanly Warfare'. For official security purposes, various branches, and sometimes the organisation as a whole, were concealed behind names such as the Joint Technical Board or the Inter-Service Research Bureau.

SOE had started its early life by being formed from a number of British Government secret departments and military units; most notably Section D from the Secret Intelligence Service (SIS), the War Office's General Staff (Research) unit (later renamed Military Intelligence Research), and the newly formed Independent Companies. One of the officers responsible for creating SOE from the ground up, and who would later go on to become its last Chief, was Major Colin McVeigh Gubbins.

Gubbins was a former officer of the Royal Cavalry and had been recruited into Military Intelligence (Research) in the late 1930s. In 1939 MI (R) was under the command of Colonel John Holland, an officer from the Royal Engineers, and was based at its cover address of 7 Whitehall Place. MI (R)'s brief was to develop new techniques in the art of guerrilla warfare and insurrection. It also acted as a think-tank for unorthodox equipment development to aid operatives in the art of industrial sabotage and black propaganda.

Gubbins had been one of its shining stars and had been given control of one of MI (R)'s most important overseas stations—Poland. However, with the outbreak of war he was called back to work on the upcoming Norwegian operations. One of the concepts that MI (R) had promoted was for a series of small, specialist independent units to attack at the rear flanks of the enemy—to harass rather than attack head on. These specialist troops would later evolve to be the military's Independent Companies. The Independent Companies had been christened the Commandos, as a respectful nod to the Boer Kommandos from the Boer War, and the name was to remain in perpetuity.

Gubbins had been in command of several elements of the Norwegian attack plans codenamed 'scissor force' and had used 'butcher-and-bolt' raids against enemy positions. He also used these small raiding groups to gather useable intelligence for any forthcoming large-scale invasions and he had seen first-hand the benefits of using these commandos for strategic attack purposes.

Upon returning to England, Major Gubbins had been returned to control of MI (R) and given the task of forming and organising a secret unit within the home guard local defence force. The Auxiliary Units were formed in the invasion summer of 1940 and were to be a *de facto* sabotage, assassination, and subversion force in case of German invasion of the British mainland. The command structure of the AUs was based around a county structure with the most vulnerable spots of the British Isles, such as Kent and Sussex on the coast, being given the greatest resources.

The units would be split into three Special Duty Sections. The first was a civilian 'spotter' force that would conduct surveillance and reconnaissance of targets; secondly the operational patrols, which were effectively the combat units that would provide the firepower. The third section would deal with covert communications to other networks. By late 1940, Gubbins had returned to SOE control and less than six months later would take over the role of Director of Training.

Elsewhere in Britain in 1940—and at Gubbins' promotion—another group of renegade soldiers and forward-thinkers had been given control of organising a programme of instruction in the dark arts of irregular warfare for the future army commandos. Named the Irregular Warfare Training Centre, this initial special training centre was based at Inverailort House, Lochailort, in the wilds of Scotland, and was used to teach special forces troops the skills needed for operating behind enemy lines and of conducting sabotage and 'hit-and-run' raids.

It was this triumvirate of fledgling organisations—MI(R), the Independent Companies, and the Auxiliary Units—that was to become a core part of the covert and irregular war against the Nazi threat, and would eventually lead to elements of them being integrated into the physical side of SOE. In the invasion Britain of 1940, the primary strategy at that time was the physical defence of the island, with the planned invasion of Europe and other theatres very much as a secondary concern. This would later change as the war progressed, and the focus would shift to allied invasion plans.

Commando and SOE agents were both initially trained at Lochailort, partly due to the War Office trying hastily to run as many as possible through the paramilitary courses. From SOE's point of view this was completely unsatisfactory (for reasons of operational security), with their argument being that the less the two groups knew about their respective operations the better. To resolve this problem SOE set about opening several Special Paramilitary Training Schools of their own, including those at Morar, Arisaig and Glenfinnan, each working from beneath SOE's organisational umbrella and separate from the training cadre at Lochailort.

One aspect of this new type of covert warfare was the use of silent killing, unarmed combat and close quarter shooting. The prime architects of this type of training at that time were two former Shanghai policemen, William Ewart Fairbairn and Eric Anthony Sykes. When a novice to the milieu of close quarter combat enters this little world they will invariably come across at some point the names Fairbairn and Sykes. If they decide to take their study further, they may investigate the background and biography of William Ewart Fairbairn. I think it is fair to say that W. E. Fairbairn is one of the (although by no means the only), founding fathers of modern day Close Quarter Battle. However, not many seem to want to progress to find out about the other name in the close combat matrix, that of E. A. Sykes. That is to their detriment, as I believe that Sykes is in many ways a more interesting character. He is not easily defined, and had, as we will see, a more unorthodox approach to close quarter combat.

Eric Anthony Sykes was born Eric Anthony Schwabe on 5 February 1883, in Barton on Irwell, Manchester, his parents being Lawrence and Octavia Schwabe, German immigrants from Leipzig. In 1885 a second child would be born, Randolph. The family were commercial entrepreneurs, employers rather than employees, and both parents had a rich and diverse background. The extended Schwabe family seems to have been very active in the business sector of the industrial north-west of England since the early 1800s. As far back as 1816, there was a company called Salis Schwabe & Co. (Fashion) Merchants in the Manchester area, a company that specialised in calico, dyeing cloth, printing, and by the mid-1800s was the second most successful enterprise of its kind in the region.

In 1834 a subsidiary company was opened, based in Shanghai, named Boustead & Co., and a further subsidiary based in Liverpool, called Sykes, Schwabe & Co., went on to open offices and have connections in Hong Kong, Singapore and Shanghai. This was a partnership consisting of Gustav Schwabe and Adam Sykes.

It is interesting to note the Sykes–Schwabe connection, especially in light of future events concerning Eric's name-change during the period of the First World War. One wonders whether the adoption of the Sykes name was a nod to one of the senior partners (and perhaps family friend of the Schwabes), that the young Eric remembered from his childhood.

In 1890 the family decided to move down south to Hemel Hempstead in Hertfordshire, eventually settling in a large property, 40 Marlowes, on one of the main thoroughfares. It was here that Lawrence set up business as a commercial printer and letterman, whilst Eric and Randolph attended Heath Brow Preparatory School for boys. Upon leaving school in their teenage years, Eric started work as an office clerk and Randolph began further education as an art student (eventually taking him into a career as a commercial artist, draughtsman and lithographer).

In 1907 at the age of 24, Eric Schwabe made a most remarkable decision, and one that was to alter his future perceptions and have a dramatic effect on his life for many years to come. He decided to set sail from Liverpool and travel half way across the world to start a life in one of the most vibrantly commercial centres of the Empire. He travelled east to the trading port of Shanghai to work in one of the trading houses—a position that he may have attained through the help of his family business connections.

Shanghai at that time was a rich and diverse trading port and, along with Hong Kong, was seen as one of the trade gateways to Asia. The darker side to Shanghai was as a result of its organised criminal and gang elements, which at one point numbered over 20,000 members. Added to this were the smaller scale crimes such thievery, mugging, prostitution, illegal gambling, loan sharking—all the hallmarks of a city approaching boiling point. Murder and violence were the normal way of solving problems in Shanghai at this time.

On 10 March 1917, and with the First World War well and truly underway, the young Eric made the decision to change his surname by deed poll to the more anglicised Sykes. With much anti-German sentiment running rife in Great Britain and her colonies, it was a wise decision for a young man of German descent wanting to get on in the world and trying to distance himself from his Germanic heritage. This appears to have done him no harm and his commercial and business life flourished. Primarily he worked for a well-known trading company based in Shanghai, Reiss & Co, which in itself acted as the agents for, amongst others, Webley & Scott and Colt's arms manufacturers and less than two years later he was appointed to be the sole representative of the Remington Arms Company in Shanghai. Remington Arms was founded in 1816 in Ilion, New York and was (and remains) one of the biggest domestic arms designers and suppliers in the world. It favoured the supply of small arms, rifles—and of course—ammunition, to various police forces, military institutions and professional gunsmiths.

By the end of 1919 he had met and courted the woman who he would eventually go on to marry—Catherine Powell. Catherine was the half Italian daughter of a Reverend Brigstocke, and had been raised in Germany. This European education meant that she spoke several languages and was a teacher of music. Eric and Catherine were married on 5 May 1919 in Reno, Nevada, USA. They returned to Shanghai, and moved into a residence in Shanghai's French Quarter with Catherine's daughter Helen, from her first marriage. Five years later, a second official ceremony was conducted in Shanghai at the local consulate, after formalities of divorce proceedings from Catherine's first husband were completed.

However, it was his next meeting that was to drastically alter his life forever. In 1919, Sykes as the Remington Arms representative, was approached by an officer of the Shanghai Municipal Police, with responsibility for firearms training and equipment procurement. His name was William Ewart Fairbairn. With the First World War rolling on in Europe, there was a natural concern of an ammunition shortage, and that colonial reserves would sooner or later be requisitioned so as to keep the war machine alive. Therefore it was in the best interest of the Shanghai Municipal Police to acquire ammunition and arms from an American supplier to circumvent any embargoes or trade restrictions. This appears to have been the beginning of the acquaintanceship between Fairbairn and Sykes. Initially it was a business arrangement, but we must assume, because of a shared love of firearms and shooting, it was later as friends and colleagues.

By now Sykes had been in Shanghai for a little over thirteen years, was a successful business agent for a number of major commercial concerns, had married, and was actively indulging in his passion for shooting and hunting. He would often organise game hunting excursions for business colleagues and clients, and in 1923 he also began working for the China & Japan Trading Co. Over time, his friendship with Fairbairn was truly strengthened, and in 1926 he decided to enrol as a reserve officer with the Shanghai Municipal Police. This was not uncommon, as many expatriates offered their services as a patriotic duty. Indeed the great majority that worked for the Shanghai Municipal Police were British. Operationally, reserve officers were there to supplement the existing officers on the beat. With the influx of gang, and organised crime violence in Shanghai, there were plenty of opportunities for fledgling officers to get their hands dirty.

Probably the most famous unit with the SMP, the Reserve Unit—sometimes called the riot squad—was there essentially to act as a quick reaction force to deal with situations of an abnormal nature. This in itself could have been, and usually was, anything from a small-scale riot, to dealing with sieges, providing VIP protection to local dignitaries, to capturing armed robbers and gang members. They were a forerunner of modern day armed response units and Special Weapons and Tactics (SWAT) teams.

The RU personnel were trained in all aspects of close contact fighting, mainly with the baton, although this would later include specialist firearms teams. Sykes certainly had over thirteen years' worth of front-line experience by the time he retired from the SMP in the late 1930s, dealing with all the violence listed above, including one notorious siege situation in January 1928 in which a gang of kidnappers were holed up in an apartment and surrounded by the Reserve Unit. Numerous tricks were tried to get the gang to show themselves at the window so that a team of snipers, 'including Mr Sykes, the well-known revolver shot,' could take them out. The siege ended with all of the gang being outgunned and eventually killed.

There has always been much speculation regarding Sykes' unarmed combat knowledge and his initial training. Certainly he would have studied the art of boxing—perhaps at first during his schooldays—but most certainly later as part of his adulthood, as did many males of this period as a matter of course. From later wartime reports of people that trained under him, they commented that he had a good knowledge of the noble art. As for his other cross-training martial art skills, it is reasonable to assume that as he had spent much of his adult life in Shanghai, and Asia, he would have studied some variant of jiujitsu and judo, certainly once his friendship with Fairbairn had taken place. His further training in close combat would have been supplemented from training in hand-to-hand combat with the Shanghai Municipal Police, which by now was using Fairbairn's Defendu syllabus.

The Defendu system was the conglomeration of Fairbairn's experience and training in the Japanese and Chinese martial arts. The primary influences were from Western boxing, Judo, Jiujitsu and Chinese Boxing. Fairbairn's accomplishments in the martial arts included holding a second degree black belt awarded by the Kodokan Juijitsu in Tokyo,

Japan, as well as studying under Tsai Ching Tung, a Chinese Boxing instructor who at one time was employed at the Imperial Palace as an instructor to the royal family.

Defendu was initially created as a self-defence system for the Shanghai Municipal Police officers working the street, with an *aide mémoire* manual created in 1915 entitled: *The Shanghai Municipal Police Self Defence Manual*. The work was later promoted for the civilian market in two books penned by Fairbairn, *Defendu* in 1926, with a reprint under a new title, *Scientific Self Defence*, in 1931.

The main techniques at its core were numerous holds, strangles, chokes, trips, throws and escapes, with the primary focus being on control and restraint tactics, as would befit a police officer having to arrest an unwilling suspect. However these were backed up with a number of striking and kicking techniques that could be used to either incapacitate an assailant or to facilitate an escape. One of the main striking tools in the Defendu system was the edge of hand strike, a variant of the *Shuto* (knife hand) that is used in many Asian Martial Arts. The edge of hand can be used to strike to virtually any part of the body and generates more force in a smaller target area than a fist would over a bigger region, thus making the edge of hand an effective weapon when targeted correctly, say to the side of the jaw-line, or to the forearm.

The other main striking technique that is utilised was the 'chin jab.' This was a heel of the hand strike, swept upwards at full speed and, as the name suggests, designed to target the opponent's chin and jaw-line and causing a knock-out. Both of these techniques would remain constant throughout Fairbairn's career, and would be a core part of his Second World War syllabus and his postwar training in Singapore and Cyprus.

Aside from the intricacies of the Defendu system, there was also the practical knowledge he would have gleaned from operating against street criminals. Their tools of the trade would have been the cosh, hatchet and knife. There was, as well, the tutelage that Fairbairn received—and later incorporated into his system—of knife-fighting techniques that he had studied with Shanghai-based United States Marine Corps Officers. All of which would have been reflected in the SMP close combat training. Added to this was Sykes' expert knowledge of pistol shooting and firearms, providing a pretty comprehensive knowledge base.

However for Sykes, a dark cloud was about to form. In April 1929,

Catherine sadly lost a long battle against cancer, and Sykes was left alone and with a stepdaughter to care for. At its heart Sykes' tale is essentially a love story—the relationship between himself and Catherine—but it is one tinged with sadness and tragedy. Indeed by the early 1930s he commented that it was only his working life that was keeping him going, and that he was eager to leave Asia at the first opportunity. Perhaps Shanghai just held too many painful memories. With Catherine's death, Sykes' world was shattered in an instant, and I often wondered whilst researching this man if his wartime adventures would have been completely different if Catherine had lived. Perhaps living to a ripe old age with his family around him, and assisting in some other position with the future war effort.

By 1937 Sykes had been placed in charge of the sniper section of the riot squad, and this was obviously a reflection of not only his knowledge and expertise with all manner of firearms, but also the level of trust that was placed in him by senior officers such as Fairbairn. To illustrate this point it was Sykes' unit that was called upon in the summer of 1937 to prevent looting and general mayhem, which in itself was as a prelude to the Chinese air force bombing Shanghai. Twelve sniper and machine gun crews were there for two days to halt a possible full-scale invasion of the settlement.

There is always conjecture surrounding Sykes' Shanghai period about whether or not he was an agent for the British Secret Service. This is a diverse subject matter—and one that everybody involved in close combat history has a theory on—some of them wild and requiring a massive leap of faith, and others being much more grounded, but with no basis of evidence. My own research on the Sykes intelligence debate is this: If we look at his Second World War vetting report by the Security Service (MI5), prior to his instructor role in Scotland, there is no mention of his being an intelligence officer—official or non-official—in any British Government organisation. In reality there is no way of knowing, however I feel there would have been at least a hint in some Government files from this period, and certainly, some eighty years on, hard evidence would have been unearthed from even the most classified of files.

Instead, because of his position in the commercial climate of the Far East, and as a representative agent of two large-scale American arms manufacturers (as well as his trading positions with several other firms), he had access to much tittle-tattle, gossip and background knowledge about the Shanghai community, as well as contact with a wide variety of business, government and diplomatic personnel. This would have provided him with excellent resources for Chinese and Japanese intentions toward the colonies as a whole.

I believe that at the most, Sykes would have been used as a low-level contact and source by the local SIS or Special Branch officer to provide a picture from a local resident with eyes and ears on the ground. This would have been perfectly normal behaviour for any patriotic Englishman working and living the colonial lifestyle and wanting to assist the British Government. He undoubtedly had embassy, military, and police contacts (especially during his time working with the SMP), and it is not inconceivable that some of them had rôles as intelligence officers.

With war looming ever nearer, the two former SMP officer made moves to leave Shanghai due to the safety and security of the Colony becoming untenable, and began to head back home to England. The question that must surely be asked is what motivated these two middle-aged gentleman to potentially set themselves up in a hazardous occupation once more?

Certainly the offering of their services to the British Government provided a home and security for their families, but more than that I believe they were acting out of a sense of patriotic duty. However, even Fairbairn and Sykes were not prepared for the position that they would be given, and they had no way of knowing it would turn out to be quite as prestigious and important as it eventually did. Perhaps they imagined working with local police forces back home, or as part of the home guard. Whatever the outcome, Fairbairn and Sykes made an initial approach to the British Government enquiring about police work in Malaya. This proposal was kindly turned down, but a rather more interesting one was made to them on behalf of the War Office, as instructors to the army.

Both men finally departed from Shanghai—after sending their families ahead to Britain—on 29 March 1940, leaving on a Canadian steamship, *The Empress of Asia*, and travelling via Canada. They finally arrived at Liverpool docks on 9 May 1940. From there Sykes travelled south to stay with his brother and his family until it was clear what route his contribution to the war would take. He would not have to wait long, having been originally spotted by a military intelligence officer with connections to MI (R) and Section D. Section D (D for destruction) was a small sub-unit of SIS with a handful of European officers and operatives tasked with planning and carrying out industrial sabotage and other dirty tricks against enemies of British interests, namely the Russians. As we have seen, with the advent of war, Section D was absorbed into military intelligence and eventually became the wartime vehicle of the Special Operations Executive. SOE at that time was very much in the process of being created from the ground up, and required suitably skilled personnel to act as officers, agents and instructors. Not that SOE was to be solely staffed with professionals, indeed many of these enthusiastic amateurs came from the world of commerce and 'civvy street' with no, or little, experience of how to run covert operations. It was very much a 'hit-and-miss' affair with officers and staff making up the majority of the rules as they went along.

On 16 May 1940 Sykes was background-vetted by the Security Service (MI5), for 'reasons of reliability and employment.' Evidently he passed Government checks because after an interview with senior officers, by mid July both Sykes and Fairbairn were on their way to the newly-created special training school at Inverailort House, Lochailort in western Scotland. Its purpose was to train civilians and the military special forces in the skills of modern covert warfare prior to a supposed full scale invasion of Great Britain by enemy forces. Ostensibly under the control of Lieutenant-Colonel J. P. O'Brian Twohig, the Commandant of Inverailort House, the two men's first rôle was to set up the training and equipment process so that the close combat portion of the training syllabus would hit the ground running. It is easy to forget that the close combat lessons were only a small part of the overall paramilitary training that soldiers and agents would receive at Lochailort. Many other skills were taught including small arms, field-craft, escape and evasion and demolition.

The author has visited Inverailort House and the surrounding region of Lochailort and Arisaig, and for the purposes of training military and quasi-military personnel in hardcore special skills the environment is unequalled. Its tough, harsh conditions are perfect for conditioning self-sufficient special forces personnel. And while many of the instructors were the very elite of the British military—including William and David Sterling, Lord Lovatt, Peter Fleming and Freddie Chapman—it is fair to say that they were all overshadowed by the deadly duo known as Fairbairn and Sykes.

As one of the first students, Major R. F. 'Henry' Hall has infamously recounted his first meeting with Fairbairn and Sykes, and it seems that the deadly duo were not above theatrics to get their point across. This included seeing the two ageing silent killers tumbling down the stairs of the grand house, only to land at the bottom, unharmed, in a battle crouch, each armed with a pistol and commando knife in either hand!

It is not the intention of this book to look in depth into the micro-workings of the departments within SOE, its internal politics, or even its wide scale operations. But it is important and relevant to investigate the type of training provided for agents in the field that enabled them to either survive behind enemy lines, or carry out an operation that involved close quarter assassination and sabotage. The details of Fairbairn and Sykes' infamous training methods are now commonplace, and the techniques themselves are designed for nothing more than to kill or maim the enemy should you find yourself without a weapon.

One such scenario could be that there is an agent working in the field who is stopped by a German soldier and is cornered—say with incriminating intelligence material upon his person. Rather than submit to capture, the agent decides the circumstances warrant the elimination of the German inquisitor. Checking there are no witnesses, the agent hits to the enemy's jaw, knees to his groin to drop him, sweeps his legs out from under him, and starts aiming kicks to the head. From there he would draw his knife, cudgel or pistol to finish him off. This was close range fighting at its dirtiest and roughest.

Unarmed combat strikes such as the chin jab, edge-of-hand strike, knee and bronco kick, were used at close range so that you could knock out an enemy, grab a weapon and finish him off. Improvised weapons were anything that came to hand—a stick, a pencil, a rope, a chain, a trowel—that could then be grabbed and used to bludgeon, throttle or stab. The knife, that age-old assassin's tool, could be used to sever arteries, penetrate the heart, or for commando's removing sentries on guard, the throat could be slashed or cut-out using the Fairbairn and Sykes' Commando knife. And, of course, finally, there was the pistol for close quarter firearms work.

'Shooting to live' as Fairbairn and Sykes termed it, consisted of one-handed shooting using a crouching stance as well as instinctive aiming, rather than using the old fashioned traditional static stance coupled with using the iron sights to hit your target, as you perhaps would at a marksman's pistol shooting competition. This was utilised with 'double taps' to make sure that the enemy went down, and stayed down. These then were the core tools of Fairbairn and Sykes' methods. All of these techniques were reinforced with the attitude of attack, attack, attack, and kill.

It may seem, however, that the mindset and attitudes that Fairbairn and Sykes espoused were welcomed with open arms by the military establishment as a whole. At times this was far from the case and their methods were in no way a *fait accompli* as to how personnel should be trained. Many of the senior military establishment found the duo's techniques and tactics too extreme and in short viewed them with suspicion, trying at every turn to sideline them and frustrate their every move. Sykes and Fairbairn are known to have openly criticised and argued with senior military officers, and top brass, regarding their lazy and derogatory attitude to the levels of training and mindset needed to win a war. Of course this would have earned them no points, but nevertheless the two close combat instructors seemed to have survived and flourished despite the machinations of certain career bureaucrats.

Undeterred, for the next two years Fairbairn and Sykes continued to teach their own special brand of unarmed and weapons-based mayhem to a wide range of students, officers, agents, soldiers and civilians. However, even these two middle-aged experts in close quarter killing recognised that they could not hope to pass their knowledge on successfully, in a wide scale basis. It was just not physically possible, especially with the nature of the war expanding rapidly outside of Europe to the Middle East and Asia. What was needed was a new generation of instructors, who would go on to teach specialised skills to their own students and subsequently to new instructors and so on and so forth. Men who had taught before, had a military background, and who had that knack of being able to pass on relevant information to their students quickly, efficiently, and with confidence. They had to be architects of the mind, capable of teaching people with no concept of killing, how to kill. Which is how, by a rather circuitous route, Leonard Grant-Taylor came to this very secretive world of silent killing and close quarter assassination.

At the outbreak of war in 1939, Leonard Grant-Taylor did what any former soldier who was still fit and active did during those dark days, he monitored the news reports, had opinions upon what would happen between the two countries and then he waited, and waited, to see if it was all a storm-in-a-tea-cup that might blow over, or if it might have far reaching consequences that would see the British population taking up arms. Either way, he was a former soldier and he was ready to be called.

By this time the Grant-Taylors had moved to a new address, 15 Elm Road, East Sheen, London, and the couple had settled into a normal regime of married life. The only contentious issue was that the marriage had produced no children. Coming from a large family this was something that Sophie Grant-Taylor desperately wanted, and was used to. However it appears that her husband either was incapable of producing children, or simply had no desire to be a father. Whatever the reason, it certainly caused friction between the couple.

On 26 May 1939, the Military Training Act (1939) was introduced, which declared that all British men between the ages of twenty and twenty-one years, who were fit and able, were required to undergo military training. Those not called up under the act were required to register again under the National Service (Armed Forces) Act 1939, which was conducted by date of birth, with men being divided into numerous groups that were required to register on a specific day. Notice was given through the media, posters, BBC, radio and newspapers, detailing which group was meant to go to where, and on what date. Formal registration involved attending an employment exchange on any given Saturday. The Exchange remained open for the whole day, rather than the then conventional Saturday morning only.

Registration involved an interview with a clerk taking personal details, name, date of birth, address, educational standard, employment, with a question as to preference for armed force, and regiment. However there was no guarantee that preferences could be met for a particular regiment, and was instead based upon where suitable personnel were most needed.

Following the registration procedure, those not filtered out would be called for a thorough medical examination, and those passed fit would receive call-up papers as allocated. With the outbreak of war on 3 September 1939, the Government introduced the National Service (Armed Forces) Act 1939, which superseded the Military Training Act. This declared that all British men between the ages of eighteen and forty-one years, who were fit and able, were required to serve with one of the armed forces for the duration of the present emergency. This later Act followed the original pre-war act with deadlines, recruitment, interviews, medical assessments and finally call-up notices.

Leonard Grant-Taylor went through this process on 11 October 1940 at Number 9 Recruitment Centre in Kingston-upon-Thames, Surrey. He gave an account of his life up to that point to the recruitment officer, once again inserting several untruths including his place and date of birth and his previous military experience. He received a medical examination which placed him as 'Grade 2', meaning that he was fit for military service. The next day, on 12 October 1940, Leonard Hector Grant-Taylor was posted to No. 5 Auxiliary Military Pioneer Corps in Huyton, Liverpool. He was given the rank of Private (number—13028858), initially with A Company, but a month later was transferred to 231 Company AMPC.

The Auxiliary Military Pioneer Corps began its wartime life in September 1939, when a number of infantry and cavalry reservists were formed into Works Labour Companies. These, in October 1939, became the Auxiliary Military Pioneer Corps (AMPC). By the end of 1940 it was renamed the Pioneer Corps. The AMPC in Liverpool was based at the edge of an internment camp for foreign nationals in Huyton, and recruits were initially documented, medically examined, and provided with kit by the quartermaster's stores on the day of arrival. The very next day basic training began covering a four week period. Non-Combatant Corps (NCC), and alien personnel were received at certain centres, and a proportion of the personnel came from the British Empire, or those who had escaped Nazi-occupied Europe.

One of the important tasks that the North-West AMPC had was creating, maintaining, and supporting an infrastructure for coastal defences and the Liverpool dockland's area from German air attack. This was paramount at this time as the Liverpool docks was a main supply route as well as being a busy launching point for military personnel. Because it was essentially a labour corps, the AMPC was seen as very much a bottom-of-the-barrel unit, perhaps rather unfairly. The work was hard and back-breaking and much of the physical labour was suited to younger men.

With this in mind one of Grant-Taylor's senior officers must have read through his previous list of service and decided that a former officer could be perhaps better used in a more productive manner than of manual labour. By the December of 1940 Private Grant-Taylor had been promoted to (acting) Sergeant.

During the latter part of 1940 and the early part of 1941, things began moving very quickly for Sergeant Grant-Taylor. Firstly, 231 Coy of the AMPC was transferred down to Taunton in Somerset, then he received a commission as a Lieutenant with his old regiment, the 8th the Queen's

Own Royal West Kent's.

The 8th Battalion of the QORWK had been formed from the No. 2 Kent Group of the National Defence Companies (NDC) in the months leading up to the outbreak of war in 1939. The personnel recruited were former First World War veterans and reservists who had joined up in peacetime with the average age ranging between forty and fifty-five years old. The 8th Battalion was very much a home defence force with its soldiers guarding vulnerable positions such as ports, ammunition depots and airfields. For Grant-Taylor though, fate intervened, and he never got the opportunity to serve with his old regiment. By February he was approached with a view to being seconded to one of the special training schools (STS), set up to train both the commandos, and SOE in paramilitary skills in Scotland.

How did he come to be involved in this secretive world of irregular warfare and commandos? In late 1940, with its creation now officially sanctioned, the SOE hierarchy went on an aggressive recruitment campaign to find suitable personnel that had the 'right stuff'. They drew from the armed services staff-trained officers who had good logistical skills, and others who had specialist training in intelligence, demolition, small arms, communications, or who had served in different countries and had local knowledge and languages. This mixture of talents proved highly creative and energetic, and an effective new service was created within a few months.

Various methods of personnel recruitment ranged from talent spotting, recommendation of a senior officer, trawling through army files, and even advertisements in newspapers such as *The Times*. No files exist of Grant-Taylor's recruitment, so we may never be exactly sure who was behind it, but there is one tantalising clue that may hold the key. A very brief message was sent from a Major E. H. Baxter in January 1941 to an unnamed colonel, providing details of Grant-Taylor's First World War and postwar qualifications, details which Baxter had told the colonel in a previous communication. He finishes the note by saying that he is 'due to be commissioned shortly' to the QORWK and finishes with the question 'is he any use to you?'

There is a referee listed at the bottom of the note with the recipient address in Bracknell, Berkshire belonging to that of an eighty-three-year-old retired brigadier-general by the name of Montague Grant Wilkinson CB CMG MVO. A former officer with the Kings Own Scottish Borderers and who during the First World War was the brigadier-general in charge of the 44th Infantry Brigade. Wilkinson also later served as a Gentleman Usher to the Royal Household.

Most notably, Wilkinson had also been Grant-Taylor's senior officer during his time as the commandant of the Army School of Instruction in Tunbridge Wells in 1917, and had obviously thought that his former *protégé* could do with a step up the military ladder. Was Brigadier M. G. Wilkinson (retired) still in touch with his War Office comrades in military intelligence, and acting as an unofficial talent-spotter and mediator between two serving officers? Or perhaps it is nothing more than a colonel or retired brigadier-general looking for a batman (military assistant) for a few months from a local regiment. It is certainly intriguing.

Whatever the method used, it was certainly more in line with his previous military experience and credentials. By March, he had received a cursory background check by the Security Service (MI5) which came back as Nothing Recorded Against (NRA) meaning that he had a clean bill of health as far as the Government was concerned.

To the casual observer, this NRA may seem a little strange considering Grant-Taylor's fraudulent background, identity, and having served a spell in prison. Why would the War Office employ such a person, especially one who was involved in a secret occupation for the military? The reader should consider that at that time, at least as far as MI5 was concerned, the only types of security risks that they were interested in were those from the far-left (communists), the far-right (fascist party) and affiliations to the republican movement in Ireland. As Grant-Taylor had none of these he was classed as suitable, and was subsequently selected for a 'special appointment under the Inter-Services Research Bureau,' the cover name for SOE.

And so by the spring of 1941, Lieutenant Grant-Taylor was headed north to the region of Morar in Scotland, to the erstwhile home of the newly formed British special forces training grounds.

In the wild north-west highlands of Scotland lies the village of Arisaig, which in Celtic means 'the safe place.' It is located on the sheltered shore of Loch nan Ceall and nestles at the base of the rocky Creag Mhor mountain. In the early 1940s the area around Arisaig was sealed off and became a Specially Protected Area which was critical to the paramilitary training conducted by SOE. As we have seen, SOE's specialist training was initially conducted at Inverailort House in Lochailort, but as its operational training requirements grew, it transferred its operations to Arisaig House, with the STS at Lochailort becoming the commando training school. The area around Arisaig became the breeding ground for further SOE special training schools, primarily because of its secluded location and range of facilities, and by the end of the war SOE had ten satellite STS's (codenamed from STS 21 through to STS 25c) around Inverness-shire, with the main STS Headquarters based at Arisaig House (STS 21).

Many of the satellite schools in that area were former shooting, hunting and fishing lodges, that had been requisitioned by the War Office to provide accommodation and training grounds for fledgling agents and special units. The courses, as we know, consisted of physical training, silent killing, weapons handling, foreign weapons training, demolition, map reading, compass work, field craft, Morse code, and ambush and strategy tactics.

As a general rule each STS was used by different foreign national groups, such as Poles, French, Norwegian, belonging to each of SOE's country sections. This was done for reasons of operational security so that no operations could be compromised by another group. Instructors were also chosen to work with a designated group because of their language skills, and any specialist training that they would need to pass onto a respective group such as intelligence training or demolitions.

One of these schools—STS 22—was based at Rhubana Lodge, a former fishing lodge located on the western shore of Loch Morar, next to the start of the River Morar, and had been built in the 1860s by the then Laird of Morar, Eneas MacDonell, to serve Loch Morar.

As a special training ground, Rhubana Lodge was perfect, and came complete with eight bedrooms, reception rooms, a large kitchen and a washroom. It also had the benefit of several outbuildings for various training exercises and only one service road in which vehicles could be viewed in plenty of time. It was isolated and discreet.

In March of 1941 Leonard Grant-Taylor had taken the train north from Somerset, and arrived as a newly-commissioned lieutenant, taking up his post at STS 22 Rhubana Lodge as quartermaster.

But what exactly was his rôle was whilst at STS 22? Frankly there is little to go on, but if we look at the SOE and SO2 (operations) file that was passed to MI5 for a positive vetting check, it states that he is to be primarily employed as a lieutenant quartermaster. However, because of a shortage in personnel there was sometimes the need for officers to cover various rôles, hence Lieutenant Grant-Taylor's rôle as a Quartermaster responsible for supply of personal and technical equipment, as well as his rôle as an instructor in various disciplines, which as we have seen he was more than qualified to either teach or assist another instructor with.

During this period at STS 22, it is known that Grant-Taylor had contact with many of the agents and soldiers that passed through the military intelligence paramilitary training wing. Some were in training to go out on operations, whilst others had just returned from action and were going through a period of re-training. From these men, the SOE instructors had the advantage of getting first-hand field reports on the latest types of commando operations, tactics, method and weapons systems that had worked under fire. Even reports of techniques that had not worked could also be useful, as it gave certain instructors the opportunity to refine the said methods that were needed to be effective. There is little doubt that Grant-Taylor was privy to these tales and methods of derring-do, later going on to use several of them as examples during his time as an instructor.

Not that it was all work in the special training schools in Scotland. Whilst they worked hard, there was also the need for rest and recuperation, and subsequently playing hard. For many of the civilians there was a sense of the unreal about what they were doing—sabotage, assassination, blowing up bridges and turning them into a cross between secret agents and supermen. It could turn even the most grounded man's head. Cooped away in isolation in the Scottish highlands, there was the very real risk of cabin fever setting in—or even worse—access to copious amounts of whisky. Gavin Maxwell, later the author of *Ring of Bright Water*, and himself the Commandant at STS 22 in 1942, recounts tales of eccentrics firing pistols into the air, and tossing grenades into the streams in the sport of extreme fishing. At times it could be like a real wild-west saloon.

Sometime during the spring to summer of 1941, Grant-Taylor attended and completed the then standardised course of weapons skills for trainee instructors at the paramilitary camps in Scotland. This programme covered the usual methods of close quarter combat such as pugilism, bayonet fighting drills, unarmed combat and close range pistol, submachine gun and rifle firing.

The military is nothing but thorough when training its instructors, as it still is, and it demanded a high level of competence to ensure that these individuals were conversant in the practice of teaching both large and smaller groups of men succinctly, as well as having a comprehensive knowledge of the subject matter. In short, it was teaching them to become teachers, and this was borne out in the 'Notes for Instructors—Arisaig Area', a document which provides the fledgling instructor with useful methods of inspiring students, and helping them to achieve their potential.

Fairbairn seems to have been the main driving force behind the earlier close combat syllabus, however things changed in 1942 when Fairbairn was seconded to the American Office of Strategic Services (OSS), and spent the remainder of the war in the USA, leaving Sykes back in England to refine the training his way.

The 1940 training course would be replaced in time by the 1942 syllabus in which E. A. Sykes dropped several of the earlier unarmed techniques such as the 'rock crusher' as they were unworkable. Whereas Fairbairn was geared more towards 'control and restraint' methods, Sykes was aiming for a short and to-the-point 'knock 'em down, and kill 'em' tactic. And so it was here, in this environment of deadly strangles, covert knives, garrottes, and blackjacks, that Grant-Taylor truly earned his spurs and learned the craft that he was to pass on to the military for the rest of his life.

Meanwhile some 3,000 miles away in Cairo, British irregular operations were to finally about to come into their own. The first year of the war had been relatively quiet in the Middle East, that was until Italy had declared war in June of 1940, and had subsequently kick-started the East African Campaign.

The Commander-in-Chief Middle East, General Archibald Wavell, while effectively dealing with the Italian military attacks and occupying the East African enclaves of Ethiopia and Eritrea, decided to plan ahead. He ordered his commanders to conduct forward planning to deal with a wide range of military options that were to be conducted within the region, especially where British forces had bases such as Cairo, Libya and Palestine. A number of these options included the use of special forces, stay-behind networks and saboteurs.

And while there were many components of British intelligence in Cairo at that time such as the Secret Intelligence Service (SIS) station, the nexus point of sabotage and irregular operations was the SOE Cairo Station. Because of its geographical location, the Cairo Station had one of the biggest areas of operation which included Iraq, Libya, Egypt, Palestine, Greece, Italy, and Yugoslavia. This often brought it into conflict with its sister service, SIS, who had been running their own intelligence operations in the region for decades, and were not impressed by a new agency encroaching upon their fiefdom.

Codenamed MO4, SOE Cairo Station was based at a modern non-descript apartment block on the 8th floor of Rustum Buildings, in the Sharia Qasr el Nil district of Cairo, and was known universally by local taxi drivers as the secret building. It operated under the cover address of the Economic Advisory Committee, and at that time its chief of station was Terence Maxwell, a former barrister and merchant banker who had been recruited from the city into SOE. One of Wavell's senior commanders, Lieutenant-General Barker, was ordered to estimate the minimum requirements for the internal security of the British mandate of Palestine, as well as a number of secret projects to set up a range of 'stay-behind' groups, intelligence networks and 'fifth columnists' and keep them active for as long as possible. However they first needed to be competently trained in all the covert skills needed to run a modern force of resisters, and the most likely service able to provide this function was SOE.

Operational experience in this type of warfare and lack of trained personnel in the area was extremely limited. This was due to the conflict mainly being active in western Europe, rather than the Middle East up until that point, which meant that MO4 was required to communicate back home to SOE's headquarters at Baker Street, London, for advice on what level of assistance was needed. Baker Street's response was swift. They would recruit and form a small team consisting of six officers and six NCOs that specialised in the techniques of 'unarmed combat, demolitions, pistol and knife-fighting, and map reading, and to instruct special parties of Allied troops in these subjects on sound English lines'. This team would also have the responsibility of establishing a new special training school in Haifa, Palestine, which was to be codenamed STS 102.

SOE Operations (SO2) branch then set about finding such a man to lead and run the team. The most obvious location to find such an officer would be in the paramilitary camps to the north, someone who was conversant with the latest methods of silent killing and close range firearms training, someone who had a proven track record as an instructor and officer, and someone who was of an age that he was able to provide a level of flair and gravitas to be able to impart this information. And so on 29 August 1941 newly-promoted Captain (Acting Major) Grant-Taylor and his team embarked on a troopship leaving from the port of Liverpool, and set sail for a period of adventures and action in the Middle East. It was to be the last time he would see his homeland, for he was never to set foot on English soil again.

CHAPTER FOUR:

A Brief History of Point Shooting

Fast is fine, but accuracy is everything.

Wyatt Earp

Whenever you get into a row be sure and not shoot too quickly. Take time. I've known many a feller slip up for shootin' in a hurry.

Wild Bill Hickok

Occupied Europe, 1942

The Officer approached the darkened door, its frame marked out by a thin seam of light that came from the light emanating from the room's interior. It was the room where murder was about to be conducted. The killing room!

He paused, took a slight inhalation of breath, held it and listened. Aside from his shallow breathing the only other noise was the sound of people talking in hushed tones from the other room, occasionally a clink of glasses or a scraping of chairs as people moved around … perhaps the faint sound of a tune from the gramophone.

But that was wrong. They were not people, for that error his instructors would have admonished him. They were targets, bodies already dead, lumps of meat. Cadavers. They just did not know it yet.

To call them people was to humanise them, and to humanise them led to hesitation at the crucial moment. Hesitation could lead to capture or death for the officer, and that could not be allowed to happen.

The weapon sat heavy in his hand. A broadsided Colt.45 semi-automatic pistol that he had cleaned, oiled and loaded himself that very morning. It was his friend, and he was as familiar with its contours and touch as a man was to his lover. He was only twenty-five and already classed as a veteran of combined operations. He had seen friends die and been wounded twice. He had been at the jaws of death and come back out alive.

And now here he was again attached to an organisation that dealt in administering death up close and personal. That was what he had been chosen for, what he had been trained for, and what he had become good at. His focus returned back to the room. He lifted his watch close to see his face to see the dials in the gloom. 10.44 p.m.

Sixty seconds left before he could enter the room and finish the 'job'. Tick, tick tick, tick … he could here the minute noise from his wristwatch resonating in his head. Sixty seconds felt like an hour.

He took a breath and reached for the door handle. Brass, heavy and he felt its weight in his hand as he twisted it and gently pushed the oak door open. He entered, letting the door close naturally behind him under its own momentum. He was instantly aware of a dim, gloomy room with old heavy furniture and three distinct figures each in a different quarter of the room, like sentinels.

The first German, he did not even see, merely sensed the man's movement. A twitching of the German's elbows, perhaps he was going for a concealed weapon under the table. Either way he had started to move and therefore think and he had become a threat—he was to die first.

The officer pointed the .45 at the German, firing from a low down centreline position, what his instructors had called a 'close hip' position. He pumped the trigger. BANG … pause … BANG. Before he was even aware that the German had taken the rounds to the head, the officer was already turning smartly to his left at the next nearest to him on the other side of the door, a sergeant judging by his uniform and pips. Two more shots at point blank range, BANG BANG, to the chest dropped him.

The third German was standing over by the window, no more than 7 feet away, with a tray of drinks. He was stood frozen as if in shock, his mouth agape. The officer punched out the pistol to full arm extension firing as he did so. Both rounds shattered the glasses on the tray, sending shards of glass flying up into the face of the third German, even as he was flung back dead against the doorway. The whole shooting had taken no more than ten seconds. The officer turned calmly away from the abattoir that was the German's room. He gently opened the door and stepped out into the darkness of the hallway.

Almost immediately a glaring light came on, illuminating the officer, who looked up, squinting at its source. Instead he saw a silhouette approaching him—small, rotund, a confident stride.

'Nice work Captain.' A deep basso voice, that hinted that its praise was begrudgingly given.

'Thank you sir,' said the officer as he started the process of making safe and clearing the Colt. He glanced down at the instructor, a major. He was small bespectacled and portly, but with a bombastic edge that told you that he meant business.

'Except, Captain, except for that pause that you let yourself have with the first target. We double tap quickly for a reason—that pause could have cost you your life and allowed your enemies to interrupt your attack! What are you the quick or the dead?'

The Captain frowned. He knew that the major, his instructor, was right and nodded in understanding. This was his final training session, and by the end of the week the captain would be dropped behind enemy lines in Yugoslavia to link up with the partisans.

He would not reach his twenty-sixth birthday.

We should at this point take a pause, and look, in closer depth, at the methods of close quarter pistol combat that Grant-Taylor learnt, studied and taught to his students. We also need to reflect on his history with firearms training and how much was his own influence and how much came from the Fairbairn and Sykes methods.

Contrary to popular belief, and despite the pushing of an agenda among certain people inside the Second World War close combat milieu, point shooting did not originate during the Second World War, and certainly did not originate with W. E. Fairbairn. Fairbairn certainly advocated it strongly, but in this respect he was not a pioneer.

Indeed, as long as man has been able to take control of a projectile weapon—from cavemen throwing rocks, to archers on the battlefield and muskets, to revolvers and automatics—gunmen have been drawing, pointing and firing without using the sights as an aiming mechanism.

Nobody told them to do this, it was, to coin a current phrase, purely instinctive shooting.

It is worth defining the terminology used between sighted fire and point shooting to give us a clear definition. Sighted fire could be classed as the exponent using the sights to align them upon the target within a time frame before pulling the trigger. Conversely, point shooting uses un-aimed shooting with no sight index, instead relying on body aiming and indexing at close range. There are numerous debates about which system has the most merit, or is the better option for a real world close combat encounter, and they are usually propagated by people pushing a certain agenda. However, for the purposes of this book we are looking at the Fairbairn and Sykes—and subsequently the Grant-Taylor—method of close quarter point shooting, and so we should spend our time reflecting upon that discipline.

I have heard people explain in great and intricate detail how one should train for point shooting, almost turning it into a great mystery that requires some in-depth level of experience involving years of practise and insider knowledge. It is nonsense. Point shooting by its very nature—should be and truly is—a simple exercise. Because it is simplistic, and because it works in the correct context, that is its benefit, and its beauty, and why it is one of the fundamental tenets of CQB. When I was first taught the basics it took a thirty-to-forty-minute session to explain the details and principles. No more than that. No great mystery, no great soul searching. After that came the hard work of practice.

If we accept that Grant-Taylor was taught, and later went on to teach, a variant of the techniques that W. E. Fairbairn taught, then it is worthwhile to go over the material covering the basic principles of what he termed 'shooting to live' and how he came to these conclusions.

The first question that should be asked at this point is: was Grant-Taylor taught the skills of close combat and instinctive shooting personally by Fairbairn and Sykes? There is no written confirmation of this or indeed even eyewitness accounts of them meeting, but we should remember that Fairbairn and Sykes were very much active in paramilitary training during this period at the SOE and commando training bases in Scotland. From early 1941 Fairbairn was based primarily at the special training school, Inverailort Castle, teaching his specialist close combat programme. So it is not inconceivable, indeed it is very likely, that Grant-Taylor attended one of these training programmes where Fairbairn was the instructor.

What is certain is that Grant-Taylor was very familiar with the methods of close quarter shooting that Fairbairn and Sykes espoused, a method that had stood the test of practical application, and had subsequently been rolled out throughout the special operations and military units of the time. There has also been the argument from certain parties that Grant-Taylor had developed his own shooting method, independently from the recognised training of the Fairbairn and Sykes method. It is an attractive idea, and certainly one that Grant-Taylor in later years encouraged with tales of being taught by old-style Western lawmen and subsequently instructing the FBI in this method during the 1920s.

As for inventing his own style of pistol shooting, that seems to be in doubt. Certainly none of the families that he had married into saw any evidence of this in his civilian life. In his later wartime SOE interview file, in the section listed as 'Special Knowledge' he states that he is technically proficient with a revolver and pistol, and that his hobbies are cricket, revolver shooting and chess. This seems perfectly possible as during the 1920s there was no firearms licensing as there is today, and many veterans of the First World War brought home souvenirs such as revolvers and pistols liberated from the Germans.

However it should be remembered that there is no evidence that Grant-Taylor was anything other than a wartime exponent of firearms, and at most an enthusiastic amateur shot during his non-military periods. We know that during the First World War he had completed the standard revolver shooting and musketry course, and continued at least some basic firearms training, probably rifle, as a volunteer instructor during the 1920s.

What seems most likely is that he had simply taken the basic weapon handling skills from his previous military service, as well as the skills he had acquired at Arisaig during 1941, and adapted them to suit a wider range of students. So whilst the fundamental principles remain the same, Grant-Taylor simply put his own spin on the method of instruction, to make it more accessible to a wider audience.

Returning to the question of the source of the SOE close combat 'shooting to live' style, how did Fairbairn come to this method of pistol shooting? William Fairbairn began his firearms career like most former military men—by being taught basic rifle handling and range drills during his time in the Royal Marines in the early 1900s. In 1910, after joining the Shanghai Municipal Police department, he became qualified as that department's musketry and drill instructor, causing him to start his learning journey to find a practical method of close combat shooting for the SMP units, specifically with the pistol.

Up to that point, the standard practice was the antiquated method—similar to what was found in competition shooting—duelling style side stance, carefully placed single shots, with no thought given to the effects of fear, adrenaline, or the conditions that the affray might take place in, which was quite often in a dark, crowded space with criminals shooting back at you.

Fairbairn set out to refine his material regarding firearms work and began a period of research that was to last nearly twenty years. He studied the latest journals, articles, and other police force accounts of armed confrontations, and seems to have been very keen to see what other people were doing regarding technique and training methods. By this time of course, the First World War was at its height and the British Army had to deal with close quarter combat on the ground among front-line troops. It was a rapid learning curve for the Tommies. Grenades, knives, coshes, and of course firearms were all being used in trenches and tunnels along the Western Front. It was fighting at bad-breath distance in often less than perfect conditions for a clear shot.

It soon became apparent among officers and weapons instructors that some new tactical methods needed to be implemented, and many far-sighted soldiers were pushing for the introduction of instinctive fire into the army's training programme. Despite this there was still a considerable amount of opposition within both the military and shooting community that denigrated this new system as being nothing more than a fad and not the way that people should shoot firearms, certainly not those in the British Army. It would be an uphill struggle.

Many researchers have also pointed out that during this period, several officers published articles and books on the subject, the most notable of these being Arthur Woodhouse, a colonial police officer in India, who in 1907 produced a small number of copies of his book, *New Revolver Manual for Police and Infantry Forces*. This was followed nine years later by Captain Charles Tracy, an officer with the King's Own Royal Lancaster Regiment, who because of his age was denied front-line service, and was instead sent as an Instructor to the Musketry School at Bisley, where he had the opportunity to experiment with his ideas. He wrote two manuals on the use of the revolver for combat: *Revolver*

Shooting in War and *The Service Revolver & How To Use It,* both published around 1916.

The Charles Tracy connection is interesting, as many years later in an interview for an American publication, Grant-Taylor acknowledged that he was taught how to handle a gun as a small boy by a man he names as Charles Tracy a Montana cattleman. Could it be that he had indeed met the real Tracy on a training course at Bisley or one of the frequent refresher training sessions for the military? Or perhaps he studied Charles Tracy's 1916 works on the subject, and had simply attributed the man's name to his own fictitious background story.

Finally another British officer that had fought in the First World War was one Captain J. B. L. Noel, whose first book *How to Shoot With a Revolver* came out in 1918, and was followed by *The Automatic Pistol* in 1919. All these works advocate the use of point shooting method for close range combat, and include the use of the aforementioned principles. I have no doubt that Fairbairn, and possibly Sykes, had at some point been exposed to these published works. For many students of point shooting it is these British Army and police pioneers that represent the starting point of what Fairbairn would build upon, and incorporate into the characteristics of what is now codified as the 'instinctive fire' method.

In 1919, Fairbairn began to expand his knowledge even more by going on a sabbatical and being loaned to the New York Police Department (NYPD). This was not just an excuse to gain knowledge in firearms and riot control work, but to observe every facet of how the NYPD operated. It also gave him access to the way that the New York Police went about its firearms training and how they conducted themselves on armed operations on the street. There is also the very real possibility that Fairbairn was exposed to FBI shooting methods during this period as many of the NYPD regularly worked with the FBI and had either been former NYPD themselves, or trained with them at the ranges. The experience seems to have had a positive effect on Fairbairn as during the six week period he was there, he seems to have been networking furiously to gather friends and contacts with a view to benefiting both the American and the Shanghai Police. Evidently this visit gave him a ream of ideas from which to work on to advance his method of shooting and police control tactics.

Less than a year later he was furthering his practical knowledge even more when he attended the British Army's Small Arms School at Hythe, with a view to gaining his Instructors Revolver Course Certificate. Prior to completing the course and attaining his certificate, Fairbairn was also given the opportunity to give an *ad hoc* demonstration of his 'shooting to live' method to several of the staff instructors at Hythe. They must have been suitably impressed because they encouraged him to train in his method at the ranges, before leaving ten days later with his newly acquired British Army Revolver Instructors Certificate.

All this research, study and commitment eventually culminated in the basis of Fairbairn's point shooting method being committed to paper in 1925 when he wrote the *Shanghai Municipal Police Shooting Manual*. This then was the start of the shooting system that he would continue to refine over the next fifteen years from both empirical study and front-line experience in Shanghai.

Fairbairn's method of instinctive fire was based on a few basic principles. But first, the basic premise of 'pointing sense' should perhaps be explained by Fairbairn and Sykes themselves. In their later 1942 book *Shooting to Live*, they recommend that the exponent try a little experiment to adequately get across the simplicity of the method:

Whilst sitting at your desk, imagine that you are holding a pistol in your right hand. Sitting squarely and keeping both eyes open, raise your hand from the level of the desk, but not so high as the level of your eyes, and with a straight arm point your extended forefinger at a mark directly in front of you on the opposite wall. Observe carefully now what has taken place.

Your forefinger, as intended, will be pointing to the mark which you are facing squarely, and the back of your hand will be vertical, as it would be if it actually held a pistol. You will observe also that you have brought your arm across you until your hand is approximately in alignment with the vertical centre-line of your body and that, under the directing impulse of the master-eye, your hand will be bent from the wrist towards the right.

In short, at close range if you can point at it, you can hit it. Fairbairn and Sykes also add, 'the elements of that little experiment form the basis of the training system' and that 'we cannot claim that the system produces nail driving marksmanship, but that is not what we look for. We want the ability to hit with extreme speed man-sized targets at very short ranges under difficult circumstances. Nail-driving marksmanship will not cope with such conditions.'

The context in which it is applied is also very important. For instinctive or point shooting to be effective it has to be used within the right range, generally accepted at anywhere between three and fifteen feet, especially with a pistol. Anything further out than that and a traditional two handed grip and aim would be more beneficial as it provides both stability and time to align the 'shot.'

Following on immediately from this is the 'quick draw'. The quick draw is the rapid movement to present the weapon to the target as quickly and as smoothly as possible. At this range, the weapon is a weapon of attack rather than one of personal defence, active rather than re-active, so the faster the draw the better the chance of the gunman getting off the first few shots and living.

The next important physical element is what is termed the 'battle crouch,' and it is borne of a natural physical and emotional response to make ourselves into a smaller target when we are threatened, or in a dangerous situation. Our knees bend, our hands come up to guard our face, and we generally lower our profile from the upright position. Except on this occasion the natural response actually assists the gunman to be, conversely, aggressive. The body crouches and leans forward, square on, aggressively, with the offhand (the non-weapon hand) being used to open doors, manipulate, cover the head or strike. Fairbairn often used the phrase 'knees over toes' to accurately describe the foot position needed for an effective battle crouch, thus giving balance and mobility.

Next are the firing positions. Fairbairn taught three basic positions; the straight arm, the three-quarter hip and the close hip. They can be moved up and along the centreline to either expand or retract depending on the range that is needed. As a general rule of thumb for modern combative point shooting I teach that the closer the target is to you, then the closer the weapon should be to your body, and it is generally accepted that the close hip is a retention shooting position for when the target is within the one foot range.

Technically speaking however, the Fairbairn system cannot truly be called instinctive shooting, as it relies on the brain to consciously move the shooting arm to a pre-determined index position, such as the three-quarter hip, thus ruling out any instinctive application of drawing and firing from a random position. Instead a more correct term is simply point shooting. The convulsive grip is an integral part of the process, as it is when the gunman has to finally fire. This is not the calm and patient gentle squeeze of the trigger of the competition shooter, but rather the violent squeeze of the whole hand. The wrist should be kept locked and tight and the whole hand convulsively squeezes the grip and the trigger, as if almost 'punching the bullet' out of the gun. Double shots were recommended, requiring the gunman to fire off at least two shots in quick succession—BANG, BANG—without a pause. Once again the rule of thumb was that you kept firing until the target was down and no longer a threat.

These then are the basics of Fairbairn's approach to point shooting. However once a method is learnt it has to be practised again and again and again. From this starting point Fairbairn took steps to improve the level of training required for the men under his command, trying to develop it until it reached as near as could be to actual combat conditions. The early SMP ranges were pretty standard fare by all accounts, but under Fairbairn's direction this was updated to include walk through ranges complete with moving targets and shoot and no-shoot scenarios for innocent civilians. This also included the use of an assault course that the officer had to run through consisting of a scramble over stiles, across pits, over barrels, up a rope ladder and down, across weighted planks and then a fifty yard sprint. This succeeded in raising the heart rate and getting adrenaline flowing throughout the body before making it to the shooting range, drawing the weapon and firing—and hitting—a number of targets, some static, some bobbers and some runners.

The final part of this evolutionary process of training was the use of an indoor firearms assault course in a self contained building, what Fairbairn styled 'mystery shoots'. These mystery shoots—or houses—involved the student entering a darkened building and negotiating his way through a series of corridors and rooms. Shoot and no-shoot targets would present themselves and the officer would have to deal with any threat appropriately.

A variety of scenarios could be designed and run within the mystery rooms, ranging from storming an opium den to catching a dope dealer, to chasing an armed criminal through a darkened building so as to conduct a hard arrest. In these scenarios criminals could be shot, but the unbreakable rule was that innocent bystander targets were to remain unharmed. The officers that were put through the mystery house shooting range were encouraged to take it seriously, with Fairbairn making it clear that it could make the difference between life and death.

> This sort of thing is not mere play-acting. It is done with the sole purpose of making practice as realistic as possible and of stimulating interest. If the men are kept indefinitely at the same dull routine they will lose interest, and results suffer accordingly.

The type of scenario-training that Fairbairn introduced within the SMP obviously had a positive effect. It gave the men confidence in their skills and aptitudes, and from 1927 onwards had become a standardised part of the SMP training and was invaluable to the SMP Stop-and-Search Squads that were shooting to live for real on the streets of Shanghai.

Another important part of the training department's curriculum was the introduction of new weapons and equipment—most notably the Colt .45 and the Thompson sub-machine gun. During his sabbatical with the NYPD Fairbairn had the opportunity to see at first hand the benefits of the heavier calibre .45 Colt and the rapid fire Tommy gun. Both weapons had earned their spurs in the battle against 'gangsterdom' in the USA in the 1920s and Fairbairn reasoned correctly that both would work well with his shooting to live method in Shanghai.

With the outbreak of war, and when Fairbairn and Sykes began their work for the Army in 1939 and later SOE in 1940, they simply transferred the basic skills, weapons and scenario training, adapting them to what was required for this new form of covert warfare. The rules of engagement that Fairbairn taught for the SMP were for personal protection and apprehension of the criminal, with lethal force being used as a last resort. For the commandos and special operations agents the operating method was to kill first. Taking prisoners was not always an option.

It is clear that these fundamental instinctive fire methods evolved from the Wild West frontier gunmen through to close quarter trench warfare during the First World War. Thereafter they further evolved through the police fighting organised crime gangs in the 1920s and '30s in the USA, and throughout the colonial police forces, such as Shanghai, right up until the paramilitary camps in Arisaig during the Second World War. It has a long and battle-tested lineage. These then were the tools, methods, tactics, techniques, and equipment that Major Grant-Taylor and his team took with them in late 1941 in order to spread the knowledge to the irregulars soldiers of the Middle East.

CHAPTER FIVE

Palestine:
Hector's 'Pistol' School

1942-1944

Hate doesn't make a good gunman. It's the man with cold precision that I want—like the American gangster.

Major Hector Grant-Taylor, 1944

The twelve-man training team led by Major Grant-Taylor arrived in Cairo on 3 October 1941 having been flown there from Durban. The team consisted of Major Grant-Taylor as Commandant and Chief Firearms Instructor, his deputy officers—Lieutenants Houseman, Thornton, Read, Eliott, Hlaux, with each being responsible for a section of the training, and being assisted by an NCO. Special Training School 102's location was in the grounds of an abandoned monastery that had been requisitioned, and was set upon Mount Carmel in Haifa.

However, upon arrival the team discovered that all was not going according to plan. They were immediately informed by a senior operations officer within military intelligence Middle East Forces, Colonel Terence Airey, that in the interim period while they were travelling to the Middle East, GHQ Middle East had grown impatient and insisted that G (R) Military Intelligence, immediately install their own men and facilities, albeit on a temporary basis.

The school's new commandant was Major Henry J. Cator. Cator, a former officer of the Royal Scots Grays and a veteran of the Western Front in 1915, was Colonel Airey's second in command, and had made moves to set up the school despite having no training in this new form of combat and warfare.

Not to be outdone, Grant-Taylor and his team travelled up to the STS, accompanied by Major William Alexander Evering (the Lord) Amherst of Hackney, who was also attached to military intelligence under Colonel Airey. The purpose of the visit was to scout out the location, and give advice on the necessary equipment and layout of the training school so that it could accommodate outdoor shooting, CQB buildings and demolition ranges.

Upon arrival, Grant-Taylor was informed by Colonel Airey that Major Cator would remain as commandant of the school, thus giving him overall command, whilst Major Grant-Taylor would in effect be demoted to chief instructor. Grant-Taylor kicked up a fuss and vehemently pointed out to the colonel that this was contrary to SOE London's original intention. Baker Street wanted a combined commandant and chief instructor at the school, more so one who had been through and had proved himself capable of delivering instruction in the latest special operations style warfare training programmes.

Obviously Baker Street wanted their man on the ground, whilst Middle East Forces Cairo demanded that Major Cator was to lead the STS, thus giving the Middle East station a greater influence about content, training and who was to be taught at the school. Inevitably a turf war ensued. This was nothing new, as GHQ ME was constantly trying to poach and requisition SOE bases, agents and operations. It was an on-going battle of wills.

Colonel Airey cabled SOE London with plans to continue the school with Major Cator in the commandant's role, but London stuck to its guns and 'instructed the mission to proceed with its work as originally instructed.' The bureaucratic battle-lines had been drawn, which consequently left STS 102 in a bit of a flux.

On 15 November, Grant-Taylor and his team travelled back to STS 102 as per London's instructions, but were stonewalled by Major Cator who would not permit them to do any work or take part in any training. The team were also not allowed to see any communiqués either to or from London. They were effectively blind and without a rôle. It was the classic bureaucratic death by a thousand cuts. Not that STS 102 was awash with students between November 1941 and January 1942, far from it, with the only exception being that of a team of undercover Greek agents that were based in an old crusader fort in nearby Athlit that had come over for a few days training. It was a school in name only.

In January Colonel Airey decided to chance his hand in the on-going battle with SOE London about who had control over STS 102. He sent a cable direct suggesting that the special training school should be increased in size and moved to a new location that would include a 'fifth column school for up to 125 trainees increasing in number later and attached to it will be the signal school.'

Of Major Grant-Taylor, it was suggested that 'Major Grant-Taylor will be employed as chief instructor' and 'will be free to utilise his instructional abilities.' Grant-Taylor, after months of inactivity stuck in the Middle East, appeared on the face of it to be willing to go along with Colonel Airey's proposal. It would at least get him and his team working again. London's response was nothing if not expected, and quashed Airey's proposal straight away.

By February, Grant-Taylor was weighing up his options about returning home to Britain or taking a staff post with Middle East Forces. Neither seemed desirable, but he was left with little in the way of options. A cable sent to SOE London dated 18 February 1942 stated that Grant-Taylor 'requested to be sent home. He feels his qualifications could be more quickly and suitably used in England.' From that point on, cables flew thick and fast in order to resolve the long-standing Grant-Taylor–STS 102 debacle.

The situation eventually resolved itself through Major Cator being found another job within MEF and his adjutant Captain Ellerbeck being promoted to Major, and in turn becoming the commandant of the school. However, ever the career realist, Airey waited until Grant-Taylor was on a troop ship back to Cairo before pushing the promotion through, lest another hornet's nest was stirred up again and Grant-Taylor should feel slighted 'through no fault of his own.'

As for Grant-Taylor's fellow team members, they were scattered across the Middle East. Lieutenant Houseman remained at STS 102 as a storekeeper, Thornton received an admin post in Tehran, Read was placed with G (R) in a local office, Hlaux was returned to his parent unit and ended up being operational in the western desert, and finally Elliot was captured and spent the rest of the war as a PoW.

As for Grant-Taylor, he was reduced from the rank of Major to Captain and remained in the region, ostensibly operating from SOE Cairo until someone could find something for him to do. For Grant-Taylor, it must have been a very frustrating time. Here he was a suitably qualified SOE

Instructor, probably the only one of his kind in the region and no one was making any use of his skills and knowledge. Not to be outdone and determined to get back into the war, Captain Grant-Taylor set about networking and using his charm, enthusiasm and knowledge to carve out a role for himself, one that could utilise his special skills.

One of these career excursions was the result of a chance meeting, which occurred in the spring of 1942. The story goes that the then Inspector General of the Palestine Police Force, Major Alan Saunders, was dining at the King David's Hotel in Jerusalem in 1942, when he bumped into an unnamed friend who was also dining there that night with an acquaintance, one Captain Grant-Taylor, who had up until that very week been teaching the Arab Legion his arcane pistol skills.

According to the legend, by the end of the short conversation, Saunders was so impressed with Grant-Taylor's personality and knowledge of close quarter pistol shooting that he immediately applied to have him temporarily seconded for the purposes of training Palestine police officers in the latest close combat shooting skills. The Palestine Police Force (PPF) was to be one of the last bastions of British colonial rule. It had been established on 1 June 1920 to protect the British mandate in Palestine. Its role was varied as one would expect of a colonial police force and initially its officers were engaged in routine criminal police work. During the 1930s it also extended its remit to include counter-insurgency operations to counter both Jewish and Arab extremism, with the most infamous of these being Orde Wingate's Special Night Squads. At the start of the Second World War the Palestine Police Force was also given responsibility to conduct military operations both within Palestine, but also in neighbouring Syria and Iraq. As such it was required to have the latest training so that it could fulfil its role.

So in late spring of 1942, Captain Grant-Taylor received permission from London to be temporarily seconded to the PPF and set about instructing them in his close quarter battle shooting skills. The PPF training took place at the firearms range at the police headquarters on the Jaffa Road, and consisted of a comprehensive series of seventeen lectures for the basic principles and the use of the revolver. Further training was geared towards the use of the Colt .45 automatic and the Thompson sub-machine gun each consisting of four lectures respectively.

The preliminary lecture covered the basic principles of gunplay and the context of how those principles would be applied for the operator whether it is for a soldier, policeman or agent. The main focus of this initial part of the training programme was the understanding of the term close quarter battle—meaning the engaging into personal combat at extreme close range of no more than a few feet. This was followed by the core of the shooting to live method.

First Grant-Taylor taught the pointing sense using the body's natural ability to point at what it wants to shoot at, stressing that 'we do not sight or aim the gun, we simply point it at the objective as naturally as if we were pointing with our finger.' In this case the index finger is simply replaced with an 'iron finger—the gun barrel. Once the pointing sense was understood, the locking and tensing of the wrist was then shown so as to give stability and was then completed by a tight grip to lock the gun into place prior to firing.

Following on from this, was the raising of the gun vertically up to the target from a 45 degree angle so as to bring the weapon up to the target. In this, it was recommended that the students stand in front of a mirror and practise, practise, practise to get both the body position correct and smoothness to the vertical raise. This culminated in the actual firing of the gun. This was not the smooth and gentle pulling of the trigger as a target shooter would, but whole hand convulsive squeeze. For the use of revolvers Grant-Taylor advocated that,

> Cocking the gun rapidly and with accuracy is just as important in close quarter battle as the squeeze. You can point, you can grip, you can squeeze and you can cock the gun. You have that perfect confidence in your weapon which tells you that you can slug any target that may come before you. You are going in, you are going to do the job at hand, and you are coming out again … alive.

One of the most important aspects of the overall close combat training was the development of an aggressive mind-set, geared toward attack rather than defence, as we have seen previously in W. E. Fairbairn's teachings. But paramount was the instilling of confidence in the student and this was why Grant-Taylor excelled as an instructor.

It can be summed up by one airborne forces trooper who stated,

> It wasn't so much the shooting skills that stood out in the course, although the man was obviously an expert of his trade, so much as the

confidence that he inspired in us. To have the ability to drop an enemy combatant by using his method, as well as his enthusiasm to get across his points effectively and without sounding pompous, which for an officer was a rare thing.

Aside from the actual pistol shooting techniques, there were also the training methods that Grant-Taylor instilled in his students to make them the finest gunmen that they could possibly be. After all, once a technique is learnt it has to be constantly practised so that the individual can reach a competent level, especially with firearms training which is a degradable skill, and in this Grant-Taylor's methodology of applied training was revolutionary for its time.

He would start with constant 'dry-fire' practice, drilling into his pupils the need for smooth body positioning, draw and firing motion. This was usually practised in front of the instructor on the range or in front of a mirror so that the soldier could notice any minor quirks and subsequently correct them.

Attention was then turned to live firing. On his courses, Grant-Taylor's students would, at his insistence, expend large amounts of ammunition to get accurate hits. The mantra was 'fire and correct, fire and correct, fire and correct,' working on them until they could accurately hit the target a minimum five times out of six. It was not unheard of for the ammunition tally to reach well over 500 rounds per student per course.

Once the students had reached an acceptable skill level, he would move the training on to give the pistol work a context. For this he would introduce his 'execution shed' and tutor them in the details of entering a hostile environment at close quarters, namely room combat. Grant-Taylor taught two methods of entering a hostile room. Firstly there was the covert approach where the target room is approached quietly, covertly, and the door is opened normally without hurry or commotion. The gunman simply steps inside, closes the door behind him and quickly appreciates the situation at hand in a split second. Alternatively there was the crash method when the gunman simply stormed into the room providing shock and awe, double tapping each target before making a quick escape. With both of these methods, Grant-Taylor enforced that the gunman should dominate the room, closing down his targets quickly and ruthlessly and that he 'must be in a position to convey [to the target] superiority and mastery of the situation.'

The point of domination is vital as it allows the gunman to instantly evaluate the layout of the room. There could be a myriad of different scenarios happening in that room at any one time. It could be dark, it could be light, there may be multiple targets moving, or it could be noisy. It may even be that the door is locked and the gunman would have to find a different method of entry.

Regardless of all these various situations, the gunman must take an instant photograph in his mind to log all the variables. With this intelligence he can then pick the optimum firing position that provides the clearest shot to all his targets, but with little exposure to himself.

In order to achieve this effectively, Grant-Taylor's room combat method was governed by a certain set of rules once close quarter battle had been initiated. This was Grant-Taylor's CQB rule of three.

Grant-Taylor's rule of three was to:

1. Shoot the first man that moves. His brain has engaged and he is now classed as a hostile target and has therefore become dangerous.
2. Next shoot the man nearest to you that moves. They could be reaching for a concealed weapon or trying to reach you.
3. Lastly, shoot anybody else that is left if you see fit to do so.

Students would then be walked through the execution shed, with Grant-Taylor guiding them from a tactile rear position. The building contained various rooms, halls and stairways of differing dimensions and at a given moment the gunman would come across various sized targets and dummies. It was a nerve-shattering test of both the student's marksmanship as well as his tactical evaluation of the scenario inside the shed.

During the room combat phase, Grant-Taylor would also interject on occasion and pepper the lecture with snippets of tactical advice about operating in a hostile building. 'You have must have other skills too,' he said, 'the interior of a saloon, an opium den, a brothel, a wine cellar or a dance hall must be photographed on your brain in a split second before you enter. You have to make sure that there is no such thing as mutual surprise; the other guy must be surprised not you!'

He would also offer practical advice about negotiating a staircase without it making a noise; step on the side, not the centre of each step, where the boards are stronger and are less likely to creak.

The culmination of the course consisted of the student being able to hit the infamous playing card target, where they were expected to hit it at 25 yards. Right hand, left hand, it mattered not.

The Grant-Taylor PPF courses were obviously warmly welcomed and a great success as a memorandum dated 12 June 1942 from Saunders to a senior officer in the Middle East, Colonel Jennings, expresses his delight with Grant-Taylor's lectures, stating that 'he is of course a master of his job, but his manner of imparting instruction is most compelling and he packs real meat into his theoretical and practical instructions, more than anyone I know.' High praise indeed.

Following his series of short lectures for the PPF, and primarily due to Major Grant-Taylor having training commitments elsewhere, it was decided that an internal manual should be produced as an *aide mémoire* for PPF officers. In early 1943 the CQB Manual, compiled by Deputy Superintendent G. A. Broadhead of the PPF, was released. This work was the Close Quarter Battle Manual for the Palestine Police Force (revolvers, automatics and sub-machine guns).

We should at this point, take the time to study the details of the Palestine Police CQB manual as it gives us a rare written insight into Grant-Taylor's shooting and teaching methods during his time in Palestine. It also gives the reader the opportunity to see the evolution from the Fairbairn and Sykes original training and allows us to see how Grant-Taylor adapted and tweaked the principles allowing him to put his own spin on the training.

According to the preface the CQB manual is,

Primarily intended for the use of instructors [and] its object is to bring to those who have, through no fault of their own, hitherto been unable to acquire that knowledge in the use of revolvers, pistols and sub-machine guns which is so essential to the police, both civil and military, and to other well defined bodies who, in war, have to face the realities of close quarter battle.

Overall the Palestine Police CQB Manual summarises Grant-Taylor's standard course, however there are one or two notably interesting sections that bear closer examination. In the fifth lecture, Grant-Taylor raises the use of two-gun shooting, primarily with the Colt. 45. This section comes across like something drawn from a Hollywood cowboy movie, with Grant-Taylor stating that 'two-gun work requires equal ability with either hand and the stress already laid upon the necessity for constant practise with both hands will now be more fully appreciated.'

Regarding having consistent shots on target using this two-gun system he notes that, 'it is manifestly impossible to shoot at two angles outside the range of vision possessed by the eyes and it is equally impossible to shoot simultaneously at two targets if the angle between them is outside the natural point angle of the two feet.' His advice for training this method was, 'take this as your rule of thumb for two-gun work: if your feet can comfortably point to the two targets, then your guns can comfortably fire at them.'

The second point of interest is a small section on 'General Hints for Police Personnel' located at the back of the manual. It provides some tactical advice on some very early and rudimentary method of entry (MOE) tactics for police officers when storming a building that contains a hostile suspect. It finishes with a number of unarmed combat and self-defence methods that would be useful for officers on duty including gun disarms from the front and rear, the securing of prisoners using the 'grapevine' technique, as well as some basic unarmed combat strikes such as the edge-of-hand blow and the rock crusher. The rock crusher strike consists of 'placing the tip of the four fingers of your master hand against the chest of your opponent just where the ribs join. Press slightly and then bring the heel of your hand as hard as possible onto the chest. The method is dangerous and may burst the chest of a weak opponent but will always drop even a strong man.'

The rock crusher is of particular interest because it was a striking technique from the early 1940-41 Fairbairn and Sykes close combat syllabus. It was later dropped by Sykes in 1942 as being unrealistic and unworkable due to the target location, the chest area, being covered by military webbing apparel thus negating any kind of tangible impact striking power. Obviously Grant-Taylor had been out of the loop regarding the updating of unarmed combat training during 1942 and had merely included it as it had been taught on his original instructors course.

Not that all of Grant-Taylor's adaptations to Fairbairn and Sykes' system were welcomed. In particular his interpretation of the 'fighting crouch' did not suit everybody as they felt it was too 'exaggerated, almost like a fencer's lunge,' thus leaving them off-balance and with their upper body too far forward to be flexible enough to move fluidly if the occasion should warrant it.

Fairbairn's fighting crouch by comparison had more in common with the boxers stance, and involved exactly the same motion with the exception that the gunman's weight is dropped down with knees bent, rather than the upper body thrown forward with the knee almost touching the ground as in Grant-Taylor's style. Fairbairn's fighting crouch body position provides all the same benefits—smaller target, pointing with the body, resting on the balls of your feet, but with the added advantages of being more flexible if you should need to move quickly.

It was not all work for Grant-Taylor. Even during the height of the war there was still the veneer of sophistication and civilised leisure time. Cairo was one of those cities that offered a rambunctious social life consisting of parties, fine dining and dazzling night life for the discerning visitor. Throughout this time, Grant-Taylor, as a man of the finer things in life, made himself known in the social milieu of Cairo and could be quite often seen having cocktails with fellow officers from SOE Cairo station, the Army or GHQ.

This was also true of Palestine, where the British military presence had built up a thriving expatriate community since the 1920s. This social class quite often led him into an overlapping of his military activities and his recreational time. One infamous pupil during this time was Countess Hermione Ranfurly, a young adventurous aristocrat and social trend-setter who had managed to secure a job working with SOE in the Middle East. In her memoirs, published in 1994, she recounts the story of meeting and being taught to shoot by Grant-Taylor. In her book he is referred to as Abercrombie.

In July of 1942 there was the very real threat of Axis forces overrunning Egypt, and the concern was that the British would not be able to hold out against the German onslaught. The embassy and GHQ staff in Palestine were recalled to the King David Hotel for a briefing and an argument broke out about whether or not the British forces should evacuate or stay and fight. Hermione Ranfurly, in a characteristically forthright way, involved herself in a heated discussion with a small, red faced, belligerent little man wearing a uniform. Her attitude that was that capitulation was not an option and that she would fight like any soldier if need be.

The man is reported to have asked her if she could shoot. Feeling foolish, she shook her head and received a scathing offer to be taught how to shoot a pistol. The next day at the appointed time she presented herself at the firearms range on the Jaffa Road at what had now unofficially become known as the Middle East School of Small Arms, although it was often referred to by those who attended it as The Killer School.

Abercrombie, (Grant-Taylor) put her through the basics of his shooting method at the firearms range before letting her loose on his execution shed which consisted of six dummy targets for her to kill, with Grant-Taylor providing a bombastic commentary from over her shoulder.

Grant-Taylor, always one for a pretty face, must have enjoyed her company because her training continued the next day and he even allowed her to use his Silver Lady. The Silver Lady was in fact a silver-plated .38 Smith & Wesson six-shot revolver. It had a pearl handled inlay, was perfectly balanced to hold and its trigger was light to the touch. Where he had acquired it was a mystery. Speculation has it that he acquired it through a pre-war private purchase at an expensive London firearms dealer, or possibly through SOE quartermaster stores, or perhaps even through the black market. Very few people were allowed to handle the Silver Lady, let alone actually fire it during training, but for those that were, Grant-Taylor would ceremoniously induct them into the elite (and unofficial) 'Silver Lady Shooting Club.'

Either way it would go on to offer a touch of the theatrical to his lessons and would eventually become his trademark weapon. Grant-Taylor and his Silver Lady, Grant-Taylor the six-shot cowboy, Grant-Taylor the gangster gunman!

For this training session Hermione had to enter the execution shed with twenty-five dummy targets concealed around the room. First she had to complete the course with the pistol, and then once again with the Tommy gun. For her final lesson several days later, Hermione Ranfurly was required to run the same drills this time using the Silver Lady, a Browning 9-mm pistol, a Mauser and the Tommy gun. She shot at dummy targets, she had to shoot oranges off a wall and finally she was required to put six shots from the Silver Lady through a playing card at ten feet.

At the end of this exhausting training session Grant-Taylor nodded with satisfaction, 'you'll do,' he said, before presenting her with the playing card she had used as a target and signed with a flourish by Grant-Taylor himself. He evidently thought well of his star pupil, as a year later he invited her to be his assistant on a training course in Cairo for a group of senior officers.

The PPF firearms range had now become, with the exception of a small number of training courses that took place on nearby military bases, Grant-Taylor's main training venue. The word was out that there was a close quarter battle specialist instructing in the region and every regiment in town was keen to have him instruct. And so between the summers of 1942 through to late 1943, Grant-Taylor became something of a flying Dutchman around the Mediterranean and Middle East, offering his unique shooting skills and instruction to a variety of regiments and organisations.

In Palestine he ran training programmes for amongst others the Corps of Military Police, the Arab Legion's 3rd Mechanised Desert Patrol, the 4th Indian Division, the 9th Army (Field Security Police), CID Flying Squad, and an officers' course for the Coldstream Guards. Each of these training courses could last for anything from ten to fourteen days (although the courses would often be longer for officers due to busy schedules) and covered the standardised course of instruction that he had initiated with the PPF.

It seems that Hector's 'killer school' was thriving and his reputation was growing, not only among the troops on the ground, but also among senior officers. It was here in Palestine that his renown as a gunman became apparent. This resulted in him being courted almost like a Hollywood celebrity by both the military hierarchy and the Western press alike, who saw a propaganda coup in the story of a mysterious officer engaged in special services.

In August 1942, Grant-Taylor was drinking at the infamous Shepherd's Hotel in Cairo when he was introduced to an American freelance journalist and writer by the name of Frederick Sondern Junior. Sondern was scouting around for interesting stories that he could circulate back home and sell to the major American publications. So the writer and the soldier sat down over drinks to chat. Did the major have a tale to tell perhaps of his wartime work? Evidently he did because the article appeared in the *New York Herald Tribune's* pull-out magazine, *This Week* in October of 1943, under the title 'Murder is His Business' and came with the tagline, 'From American gangsters the Major learned many lethal tricks to teach his super-commandos!'

In it Grant-Taylor is not mentioned by name but is instead referred to as 'the Major,' and is portrayed as a cold blooded and ruthless international gunman and assassin. There are tales of teaching Special Branch of Scotland Yard the techniques and skills of close quarter fast shooting and of working personally with the FBI to study their pistol shooting methods. Also claims that he spent nine years working with the FBI and various police departments of New York, Chicago and San Francisco. He also recounts tales of consulting with the likes of Chicago gangsters such as Dion O'Bannon, Johnny Torrio and the Touhy Gangs about the merits of street weapons, assassinations and kidnappings. But perhaps his most infamous story in the article was how the Major led a team of commandos to assassinate six German Luftwaffe aces in France. Landing from a submarine the commando team infiltrated the area before happening upon the inn where the Germans had spent a night carousing. The Major is said to have quietly opened the door to the bar and before finishing them all with his trusted Tommy-gun.

As we now know this was all fiction, and it is fair to assume that Grant-Taylor himself wasted no time in concocting these stories rather than them emerging from the hand of an over-enthusiastic journalist. However from a positive propaganda viewpoint it was an inspired piece of work as it portrayed the British commandos as a ruthless bunch, not averse to resorting to gangster tactics and methods to get the job done against an evil enemy. In short, they were not afraid to use dirty tactics.

Grant-Taylor's other public appearance in 1942 was when he was asked to pose for a series of photographs in which he appears to be instructing the British General Officer Commanding (GOC) Palestine, Major-General D. F. McConnell CBE DSO in the use of the Tommy gun at the Middle East School for Small Arms. The photographs were taken by an official Armed Forces Publicity Unit (AFPU) photographer to record the war for propaganda purposes.

Along with the PPF manual, and the Sondern story, the McDonnell photographs are one of the few remaining pieces of recorded material about Grant-Taylor during his time in the Middle East. These vignettes then were the core of Grant-Taylor's lectures, presentations and his growing public persona among the Allied forces in the region. His anecdotes would go on to spread, grow, take on a life of their own, and inevitably be taken as fact, and it is not unreasonable to say that it was here in Palestine that Hector Grant-Taylor's legend was made.

So did the alleged combined operations to assassinate the six Luftwaffe aces and the Norwegian quislings actually occur during 1940-41? Was Grant-Taylor responsible for these assassinations?

Looking at the claims objectively, and with hindsight, it is slightly curious to suppose that a portly man in his fifties that had never passed the commando course would be chosen to run hit-and-run raids behind enemy lines, especially when there was a stream of younger, fitter men capable of fighting the war in commando style. And as for postwar tales of Grant-Taylor having a reputation as a wartime assassin being sent out on missions to dispose of enemy agents and traitors, the evidence suggests that was certainly not the case and was instead the romantic envisioning of several pulp fiction writers.

Grant-Taylor had no operational experience of commando or combined operations in the field, but he was also savvy enough to recognise that he needed to transmit his message and confidence in his firearms lectures by interspersing it with tales of action hero 'derring do'. After all why should the young soldiers in the field accept the word of an instructor that had never used his supposed killing skills in actual combat? So he did what was needed to counter that argument. He made up a range of plausible tales of his various roles in combat operations—both military and law enforcement. Nobody would be able to check them out because who would challenge an officer?

And while the evidence now points to the fact that Grant-Taylor never took part in these operations, it does not mean that they did not happen. Perhaps they happened with another officer or unit. What seems most likely is that a similar scenario conducted by one of the myriad of commando and special forces groups of the time was used as an example and extrapolated upon. One of the most likely units that was involved in this type of operation, and with which Grant-Taylor would have had knowledge of during his time in the paramilitary camps in Arisaig, was the little known Small Scale Raiding Force (SSRF).

The Small Scale Raiding Force (named No. 62 Commando) had been formed in 1941 and was ostensibly under the control of SOE. The unit consisted of fifty-five men plus officers and its operational role was to conduct pinprick raids against French coastal installations and defences. The SSRF was known for its hit-and-run attacks along the French coast as well as on the Channel Islands, with many of its objectives being to capture or kill enemy personnel at close quarters inside their own back yard.

One likely operational candidate during 1941 was Operation Savanna. Proposed by the Air Ministry, its aim was to eliminate a group of the *Kampfgeschwader 100*, an elite German Pathfinder formation stationed at Meucon airfield, outside Vannes, whose task was to spearhead night raids upon Britain. Over the previous months, these Luftwaffe aces had played a vital role in guiding German planes into bombing the city of Coventry, with devastating results. The unit chosen to complete this assassination was a group composed from SOE trained Free French Forces. It was known that the pilots regularly travelled from the airfield to their billets in nearby Vannes and it was on this deserted stretch of road that the Free French unit would launch its ambush. The five-man team was led by Captain Georges Bergé, a veteran of the French military who would later go on to form the French Special Air Service Squadron in 1942.

The Savanna team were dropped by an Armstrong Whitworth Whitley Bomber on 15 March 1941, and set about reconnoitring the German pilots' travel route at once. However it soon became apparent that the intelligence they had received was somewhat out of date, as the pilots had abandoned their bus and had instead opted for separate cars to take them to the airfield. In theory the Savanna team would only have one shot at this attack before the alarm was raised. With the disruption to their ambush now evident, the plan had to be cancelled and the Savanna team started the exfiltration process, which involved escaping by submarine, the HMS *Tigris* on 5 April. Despite Savanna's good intentions, and its request from the Air Ministry, the chief of the air staff, Air Marshal Sir Charles Portal is alleged to have rebuked one SOE officer on the ethical difference between dropping undercover spies into enemy territory and the dropping of assassins, which fundamentally is what the Savanna team were.

It would seem clear that Savanna was the prototype for Grant-Taylor's example of ambushing the Luftwaffe aces, and that Captain Bergé was the influence for Grant-Taylor's mysterious alter-ego, the Major. The fact that Grant-Taylor used these stories should not be seen as detrimental to the role he was given by SOE and the army. Grant-Taylor was a practised and expert pistol shot, he was an exemplarily instructor who knew his subject matter, he had a passionate manner that enthused his students, and he had been in combat during the First World War.

His task as an instructor was to teach certainly, but also to become something more elemental and iconic to the young soldiers and special operators that would be going out behind enemy lines or on to the battlefield to fight. He needed to be larger than life, almost superhuman and mythical so that they would trust in who he was and what he was teaching them. These anecdotes that he perhaps heard from actual commando operations were then tailored to illustrate the points that he was trying to make in his close quarter firearms training. After all, imagine the confidence boost to the young soldier who was about to storm an enemy building, knowing that he had been trained in the very latest CQB methods by an internationally renowned major of special services, who had taken down gangsters and German agents alike. In many ways this confidence-building, in both the student, and the method, was more beneficial than firing 1,000 rounds of ammunition on a range.

In December 1942 a memorandum was sent from the Middle East Forces effectively ending Grant-Taylor's current job, with a note that he should instead be found employment with other organisations that could use his skills and perhaps even receive a promotion, with the caveat that he should never be allowed to instruct 'Jewish regular or irregular troops.'

This we can see, was a security concern at the time as the British Government could not be seen to be actively taking sides in the Jewish-Arab conflict or indeed fall into the propaganda trap of having British-trained Jewish extremists attacking British forces in later years. But what to do with this maverick major that was out in the Middle East teaching all kinds of strange battle tactics to all kinds of unusual units? Where would he fit in?

The initial idea of the Director of Military Operations was for Grant-Taylor to be recalled home, receive a promotion and to be used as an SOE Liaison Officer to the War Office in London. However before this transfer could be realised, fate intervened once again, bringing with it, as it so often does, an opportunity that was to have far reaching consequences. Grant-Taylor's promotion came in early 1943 when he was transferred from SOE GHQ Middle East Forces Command structure, and posted to a holding squadron belonging to the recently formed unit operating covertly in the Middle East and North Africa at that time—the Special Air Service (SAS).

The wartime SAS had originally started life in 1941 from an unorthodox concept created by a young maverick officer who was serving with No. 8

(Guards) Commando. That officer's name was Lieutenant David Stirling. His idea was for small, independently run teams of parachute trained soldiers to operate behind enemy lines. Their remit would be to gather enemy intelligence, sabotage enemy craft and run hit-and-run raids on the enemy's supply and reinforcement routes. And while his idea was sound, actually implementing it would turn out to be far more difficult. That was until he was able arrange a meeting with the Commander-in-Chief Middle East, General Auchinleck, who liked both the plucky young officer and the idea of a mobile unit engaged in hit-and-run tactics across the desert. With Auchinleck's patronage the plan was sold to the Military hierarchy, and given the green light. Stirling's aggressive and offensively operational unit was officially known as L Detachment SAS Brigade.

From its roots in 1941 the SAS was to grow and combine elements of the Layforce Commando as well as working closely with the Long Range Desert Group. In truth, for much of its early life the SAS and the LRDG were completely integrated with both units providing both personnel and vehicles for operations. The SAS achieved astounding success running attack operations against enemy airfields, installations and convoys, so much so that by September 1942 it was renamed the 1st SAS Regiment, with Lieutenant-Colonel David Stirling DSO in command. In January of 1943 Stirling was captured during operations in North Africa and would later spend the remainder of the war as a prisoner of war in Colditz. With Stirling's departure, the 1st SAS, which was now woefully depleted, was recognised as being in need of some reorganisation.

The man who was to take over Stirling's rôle, and to conduct this restructure, was Major Robert Blair (Paddy) Mayne. Mayne was a formidable soldier; a former international Rugby player, and keen sportsman, he was well suited to the tough atmosphere of the special forces. In January 1943, 1st SAS Regiment was reorganized into two separate parts, the Special Raiding Squadron (SRS), and the Special Boat Section (SBS). Mayne was appointed to command the Special Raiding Squadron, and led the unit in Sicily and Italy until the end of 1943, where he later earned another bar to his DSO. With Mayne now in command he wanted his special forces troopers to be ready for a new type of fighting that he knew would be taking place with the invasion of Italy. Fighting that would take place in streets, buildings and forests, with men trying to kill each other from a few feet away. After an initial enquiry at MEF HQ it did not take long for the name of Grant-Taylor and his shooting methods to be mentioned as being just the thing that the Middle East SAS needed.

The CQB training took place, once again, at the Jaffa Road shooting range and execution shed. The class structure could at any given time consist of a conglomeration of special forces (SBS, SRS, SAS), Palestine police officers, and members of the Corps of Military Police. Regardless of their operational rôle, the training syllabus remained the same. Training these soldiers, Grant-Taylor immediately focused their minds with his opening salvo during the lecture session: 'This is a school for murder! Murder is my business! Not the vague shooting of unknown people in combat, but the personal, individual killing of a man in cold blood. It's an art which you have to study, practise and perfect!'

He was also not averse to showing off from time to time. He would, when the mood took him, draw the Silver Lady flick a coin in the air in a theatrical style and attempt to shoot it. As one former SAS soldier, David Williams, commented, 'he restored my belief in cowboys.'

After his success working with the SAS, SRS and SBS, Grant-Taylor was once more on the road around the Mediterranean, providing his unique brand of teaching in close quarter combat. These instructional forays included a series of lectures and training courses in 'killing with a pistol' for the 4th Parachute Squadron of the Royal Engineers in North Africa during the month of August. This was followed in October by lectures for the men of the 3rd County of London Yeomanry (3rd Sharpshooters), the 21st Independent Parachute Company, and the 156th Parachute Battalion following the Allied invasion effort in Italy.

The men of the 156th Parachute Battalion certainly had occasions to use their new-found shooting skills. Major John Potts of A Company 156th relates the time that his unit were approaching a seemingly deserted farm in the Castellanita region of Italy when they were approached by a German patrol. 'Fortunately,' he recounts, 'they were not keen to do battle, but we all took up fire positions ready to use our revolvers as recently taught by Grant-Taylor, the veteran of American gangland, who had been employed by our Brigadier, Shan Hackett, to teach his officers to use the revolver most effectively.'

In many of these training lectures Grant-Taylor, ever the raconteur, encouraged his tales of being a small arms instructor to the FBI and, with the shadow of Fairbairn and Sykes in the background, an instructor in close quarter shooting to the Hong Kong police force. This led many of the young officers and soldiers to believe that he was in fact an American army officer.

During this period in Italy, Grant-Taylor was alleged to have been invited to go out on patrol with elements of the Eighth Army. Ever keen to get into the war, this is said to have included numerous occasions of 'patrolling and infiltration work' and that the men of the Eighth Army 'thought highly of him—both operationally and as an instructor.'

A clue to where he may have taken part in these front-line forays is recounted in a postwar article in which Grant-Taylor tells of being at 'the third battle of the bridgehead' in Gioia del Colle, Taranto, in southern Italy during September 1943. Gioia del Colle was of strategic value to the Allies primarily because it was the location of a large airfield and after an aggressive Allied offensive, the Germans conceded defeat and withdrew on the night of 16-17 September.

As a final foray into the Italian Campaign, Grant-Taylor had holed up with a unit from 2 SAS led by the formidable Roy Farran. The SAS men were stationed at a requisitioned country house with beautiful, relaxing gardens just outside of Taranto. Grant-Taylor reportedly stayed with the special forces for a few days, conducting pistol and sub-machine gun CQB training during the day, and relaxing with good Italian food and wine provided by the manor's resident cook, during the evenings. Of Grant-Taylor, Farran regarded him as a first-rate teacher in his chosen art of CQB. He would start with his usual patter of his now famous quote, 'First I must tell you that murder is my business.'

He would then go on to lay out his ideas and tactics for shooting with the pistol and Tommy gun, which he quite often compared to a musical instrument! As with all musical instruments he would encourage his students to play it in short bursts—'tacktack, tacktack!'

Among the SAS, this earned Grant-Taylor the nickname 'Tack-Tack.' Farran had been ordered to conduct reconnaissance patrols and attack targets of opportunity in the area ahead of the general Allied advance. This also involved a section of jeeps from 'D' Squadron, which ambushed a number of German convoys, and linked up with advancing Canadian forces. They also became involved in street-fighting on several occasions before moving to the city of Bari, where it was said Tack-Tack Grant-Taylor's CQB training had been invaluable to the SAS.

CHAPTER SIX:

China, Burma, India: Slim's Shooters!

1944–1945

One could not choose a worse place for fighting the Japanese.
Winston Churchill

Following his excursion to Italy, Major Grant-Taylor returned to his home base of Egypt to give a series of close combat lectures to soldiers of the 4th Queen's Own Hussars, before taking a well-deserved break during Christmas of 1943. Over the past six months he had been roving from one country to the next, giving lectures and unofficially at times, being involved in front-line operations and dealing with injuries resulting from these actions. Even for a man of his fitness and energy it must have been exhausting.

The start of 1944 began with another round of lectures for the Corps of Military Police. Setting up the camp, pitching his lectures, demonstrating the pistol work, fire and correct, fire and correct, fire and correct, break camp, then doing it all again the next day on a never ending carousel. Added to which, Grant-Taylor—ever a man who liked a snifter or two—was beginning to drink too much between assignments, a potentially dangerous cocktail for a man of his profession.

In the February of 1944, the War Office received word that the King of Greece, George II of the Hellenes, was eager to recruit Major Grant-Taylor exclusively to train Greek soldiers to be his personal bodyguard and to train an *ad hoc* police force.

King George II had been in exile in London since 1941, but with the tide of the War turning rapidly toward an Allied victory, he was beginning to make plans for a return of the monarchy to its hereditary homeland, and had re-located his base of operations to Egypt in 1943. However to ensure a smooth transition, he would require the support of the British Government and its military knowledge to assist.

Cable traffic had already been passed to and forth between Cairo and London enquiring about Grant-Taylor's suitability for this prestigious appointment, with Cairo stating that he was 'acknowledged as a brilliant instructor in revolver assault.' However it is fair to say that Grant-Taylor was not universally loved by all of GHQ ME, as the same cable describes him as a 'Stormy Petrel, particularly in Palestine,' which was the very polite way of saying that he was a rebel who was liable to cause trouble at any given opportunity. This was further expanded upon with the information that 'the director of military training recently gave him an appointment, but cancelled for non-conforming with orders and failure to report for duty. He is not suitable for command from an admin point of view.' It seems that certain elements within MEF were keen to put the boot in to Grant-Taylor's future plans.

Despite this, the British Ambassador, the Commander-in-Chief MEF, the King, and the British Military Liaison Officer Colonel Humphrey Butler were all eager for Grant-Taylor's training appointment, and fully endorsed him as a suitable training officer. However the senior command, not wanting a valuable asset to be isolated in one country for a long period, had other ideas, and wanted him rapidly shipped off to Persia and Baghdad to train military personnel.

With the war in Europe and the Middle East abating thanks to the Allies' overwhelming force, attention inevitably turned to the conflict that was still raging in Asia, with the main theatre of operations being China, Burma and India

The South East Asia conflict had its roots way back in 1941 when Japan entered the war on the side of the Axis powers, with her main aims being to acquire raw materials, particularly oil, rubber and tin, and through expansion of the so-called Greater Co-Prosperity Sphere, to create space for the population of the over-crowded home islands.

The surprise attack on Pearl Harbor on 7 December 1941 was a crushing blow to the American forces. However despite this its overall aim—the sinking of the American fleet's aircraft carriers—was a complete failure.

However, this in no way faltered the Japanese schemes to continue their military plans elsewhere across the region. Soon after Hong Kong and Indo-China fell to the Japanese invaders with relatively little resistance. This was further compounded when they also secured the prize of the Malay Peninsula and Singapore, where British, Australian and Indian troops were routed and forced to surrender. Shortly after, the Japanese took the Dutch East Indies, and contained a series of small islands across the pacific, subsequently threatening the security of the Australian coast.

As for Burma, the Japanese had a two-pronged strategy; to cut the Burma Road access route to China, from which military aid was being passed from Rangoon, and secondly, the fall of Burma would place the Japanese military at the doorway to India.

The response was quick. General Sir Archibald Wavell, supreme commander of the Far Eastern theatre of operations, had two divisions, the 1st Burma and 17th Indian, that were formed into Burma Corps (BURCORPS). He ordered his commanders to defend well forward. The commanders on the ground, however, were far more aware of the practicality of the situation, and how limited Wavell's order would turn out to be. The soldiers themselves were ill-equipped and ill-trained to fight in jungle conditions for any sustainable period of time, and take on a better trained and defended enemy.

Lieutenant-General William Slim's Burcorps, fell back up the Irrawaddy river, and in May 1942 the retreat finally ended, leaving the shattered remnants of Burcorps beginning to prepare for a return to Burma. One of the operational forces used was Brigadier Orde Wingate's first Chindit expedition, in which the eccentric Wingate used stealth and guerrilla tactics in his jungle fighting against the Japanese. The Chindits adopted the methods of infiltration and reconnaissance deep within the Japanese army's own backyard, which proved to be a momentous morale boost for the Allies.

In 1943 the South East Asia Command—SEAC—was restructured with Wavell being replaced by Lord Louis Mountbatten. Mountbatten brought with him a 'new broom' and a new way of doing things, most importantly the much-needed air-support that was so vital for logistics and re-supply for the 14th Army.

With the dynamic General William Slim now in command of the 14th Army, a new ethos was spreading through the chain of command. They became more resolute, tougher and willing to take on the enemy with a gusto that would send shockwaves through the rank and file of the Japanese.

While the generals and military brass spelled out an overall strategy, for the men on the ground, fighting the longest fought conflict by the British Commonwealth in the Second World War in the dense jungle and open paddy fields of Asia, the 14th Army were slogging it out with an enemy that was nowhere near beaten in this brutal campaign. Fighting was often at close range using hand-to-hand combat, combined with the heat, rain and all the hidden dangers of jungle fighting.

An account of how brutal and vicious this type of close quarter combat was, can be found in the story of Sergeant Albert Fitt of the Royal Norfolk Regiment, when his platoon attempted to storm a Japanese bunker. Whilst storming the bunker, Fitt received a gunshot wound to the face—blasting out several of his teeth—before throttling the enemy soldier and then finishing him off with his own bayonet!

As for the Japanese, they were a lethal and an exceptionally formidable enemy, not known for taking prisoners, and who preferred the torture and execution of injured allied soldiers rather than collecting PoW's. However, it seems that the Allies were also willing to get their hands dirty, and to be ruthless when the occasion warranted. An example being that of Major Mike Calvert, then commanding a small unit intent on harassing the enemy along the Irrawaddy River. He recounts the tale of happening across a group of thirty Japanese soldiers stood around inspecting the corpse of an allied serviceman. When Calvert and his unit were in range of the gathered crowd, they emptied out their Tommy guns into the mass, killing them all, before making their escape by a fast launch vessel.

To compound these problems, the jungle itself was a soldier's nightmare come true, and the conditions in which the men had to fight and live were dire. The risk of malaria, dysentery, leeches, monsoons, lack of fresh water, and proper medical facilities would begin to take their toll very quickly. Men lived in primitive conditions and the climate itself was unhealthy with temperatures often exceeding 45 degrees centigrade, and the humidity level would often reach a swampy 98.4. These types of conditions were the breeding ground for all manner of tropical diseases. Aside from the usual dysentery and malaria, there was also the risk of prickly heat, foot rot, ringworm, and heat exhaustion.

As for Grant-Taylor, it was business as usual as word of his reputation and methods grew and spread, and in July of 1944 Major Grant-Taylor received a promotion to the rank of Lieutenant-Colonel and officially became listed as being part of the headquarters staff of the army in India. He was a general staff officer (1st grade) of the General Staff Branch, and part of the Special Duties establishment responsible for running the training teams for regiments and units in that theatre of operations. He had now become the travelling instructor for China, Burma and India, with everyone from senior officers to soldiers on the front-line wanting to be schooled in his method of tough fighting.

During the summer of 1944, Grant-Taylor arrived at Howrah Railway Station, Calcutta, where he was seconded to run a series of his lectures for the US Army in India. He was minded by a young American NCO and former news reporter by the name of Cal Tinney. Postwar, Tinney worked as a broadcaster and writer in the USA, and went on to write a short article based on his experiences working with Grant-Taylor entitled 'Hector's job was murder.' This article, while factual in many respects, also gave birth to many of the myths that have subsequently surrounded Grant-Taylor's life and achievements. As we now know, many of them were pure embellishments by Grant-Taylor himself. What is interesting about the Tinney interview, and the earlier Sondern article, is the inclusion of Grant-Taylor's thoughts on edged weapon combat.

As we know, Grant-Taylor studied Fairbairn and Sykes's knife fighting methods as a part of his original paramilitary instructor training in 1941. This involved the use of the infamous Fairbairn and Sykes commando knife, a double-edged stiletto type blade with a foil grip.

Fairbairn's system was based initially on the art of the fencer, but was backed up with real life experience during his time in Shanghai, as well as from cross-training with United States Marine Corps personnel. By the beginning of the war, the techniques that were taught covered sentry removal and knife fighting.

In the 1942 SOE Silent Killing Syllabus, the use of the knife is described thus: 'The knife is a silent and deadly weapon that is easily concealed and against which, in the hands of an expert, there is no sure defence, except firearms or running like hell.' Fairbairn and Sykes' students were taught how to hold a knife, feint, thrust and parry. The training also covered attacking the vulnerable parts of the body, deception to launch an ambush attack, concealed carry of the weapon, as well as weapon retention training. To the uninitiated, knife fighting looks almost like a genteel fencing game with the combatant darting in and out quickly, the blade constantly moving to cut, slash and stab. It is a façade. Knife combat is brutal and it is hard, hard, work that can quickly wear down both an opponent and the knife fighter. It is also a messy tactic that is not clean, silent, nor quick to take effect. It is certainly nothing like how it is portrayed in the movies. These were sentiments that Grant-Taylor seemingly endorsed on the subject of knife work; 'He doesn't like knifing; he considers it crude and unreliable, as well as unpleasant. But there are occasions when a sentry must be removed silently.' His most famous quote on knife combat is that, 'you don't stab or hack with a knife—you stroke with it.' He would then go on to display a fluid cutting motion to attack the various arteries and nerves from all angles.

This also filtered down to Grant-Taylor's thoughts on unarmed combat. Over the years many researchers have tried to attribute all manner of hand-to-hand combat techniques to Grant-Taylor, and discover what he had taught. This included some unverifiable documents from unnamed (and therefore unaccountable and potentially unreliable) sources that claimed to have Grant-Taylor's 'silent killing course' that he taught to the SAS. This SAS syllabus claims to cover attacking vulnerable parts of the body with a variety of edge of hand, chin jabs, boot kicks and chokes and strangles. It also has a section on knife usage, knife defence and prisoner handling. It claims to cover a seventeen-hour training period.

Whilst he would certainly have had to be put through basic close combat training during his initial training in Arisaig, we should remember that Grant-Taylor's role was to be a firearms instructor on his initial assignment to the Middle East in 1941-42, and it is evident that his priorities would be geared towards that particular discipline.

Of all the people who had been trained by Grant-Taylor who I interviewed for this book, none of them could confirm that he had trained them in any hand-to-hand combat methods. So while the subject of hand-to-hand combat certainly seems to have been mentioned and discussed, instead the teaching focused solely on pistol shooting. As one of his students commented, 'he was tough and hard, but not in a street fighting way.'

So while he would certainly have knowledge of silent killing methods, it seems it was not something that he practised or taught. In fact the only wartime reference to unarmed combat from Grant-Taylor was, as we have seen, located at the back of the PPF-CQB manual. The evidence seems to suggest that Grant-Taylor preferred the way of the gun rather than the use of cold steel or rough-house fighting. These thoughts lead us on to Grant-Taylor's views on killing at close quarters. As would be expected from a teacher of close quarter killing, he is tough-talking, straight-to-the-point and ruthless in his explanations to his students.

> Shooting a Jerry is like swatting a fly. Keep thinking that, shoot a few and you'll sleep like a baby even after the bloodiest shambles. Only two things will interest you—getting the job done and getting away.

As for his thoughts on the ruthlessness needed for personal killing:

> Is killing easy? No, not when the guy's at arms length. To kill an enemy at long range, with a blockbuster, a twenty-five pounder, or the sixty-eight millimetre, is a routine job. But in close quarter battle you kill at conversation distance. You can't let it get to you. You've got to be able to watch the whites of the poor devil's eyes turn up, kick him in the face in case the job is incomplete and forget him ... especially forget him.

All of which is the sinew-stiffening rhetoric that he had used in the Middle East, and would continue to use to good effect to the troops in SEAC-CBI. Whilst in India, Grant-Taylor had been temporarily poached by Major-General Gilbert Cheves, the Commander of the Army Service Forces in Calcutta. Cheves, who had a fearsome reputation for 'getting things done' and for cutting through bureaucratic red tape, had obviously received word of an Englishman who was not afraid to mix it with pistols at close quarters.

General Cheves was said to be 'captivated by him' and was keen to see that his men received training in this unique discipline. Based out of the Great Eastern Hotel, Grant-Taylor spent six months teaching various units of the American military and small numbers of Office of Strategic Services (OSS) action teams that were to be dropped or moved into enemy territory. The lectures by now were routine for Grant-Taylor, consisting of his assistants setting up several temporary ranges at various bases, conducting the training for a few weeks and then moving on to the next location.

One OSS officer, who witnessed one of Grant-Taylor's CQB lectures, was Major Roger 'Tex' Hilsman who happened to be at 14th Army Headquarters in Eastern Bengal that day. Tex Hilsman was at that time leading a unit of guerrillas as part of the OSS's 101 Detachment and was intrigued at this display of fast shooting.

In his book, *American Guerrilla*, Hilsman recalls hearing Grant-Taylor tell a number of tales of the 'old west' and more specifically about Wild Bill Hickok, the legendary gunfighter and lawman. Grant-Taylor is said to have used Hickok's shooting prowess as an allegorical example to illustrate his points regarding quick draws and instinctive firing, and related the tale of Hickock walking into a saloon and taking on five gunmen and shooting them all down.

What is interesting about Grant-Taylor's training of young US troops is how he plays up to the American psyche and furnishes his story with several Americanisms that would strike a chord with young men straight out of New York City, Indiana and Milwaukee. Gone were the tales of stiff upper lip commando officers. Now it was all gangsters, gunmen and cowboys.

The references to the FBI and the Chicago underworld had always been a part of his patois, but now there were also claims that Grant-Taylor himself had been the trigger-man that had gunned down John Dillinger outside the Biograph Theater in 1934. The shooting of John Dillinger is actually credited to Special Agent Charles Winstead, a former Texas Ranger and FBI agent that took the notorious bank-robber down with three shots. Regardless, these tales all added to an enjoyable and informative lecture circuit with Grant-Taylor acknowledging the level of influence gunfighters of the old west—both historical and fictional—had on his audience, and the popular trend of the young troops avidly reading the pulp Wild Western dime store novels of the time could only add to that.

To further hammer home the point in a theatrical showman manner, and as part of his lectures, he would talk in a slightly off kilter American west-side accent before introducing his six-shot revolver the Silver Lady and snap shooting at a nearby target. To those same young troops from New York, Indiana and Milwaukee, it must have seemed as though the gunmen from Tombstone had entered the War in the CBI. Throughout 1944 and into 1945, and almost without exception, the soldiers and officers that studied under Grant-Taylor during his time in south east Asia seem to have nothing but praise and admiration for him both as a talented gunman and an exceptional instructor, and over the years many of Grant-Taylor's alumni have gone on record extolling his virtues as a teacher of close quarter combat.

One former Palestine Police officer, that later served in CBI, recalls;

I remember Grant-Taylor. Not from Palestine, but during the war when I was in India at the Young Officers' Training School in Behar state (this was a jungle training course). He turned up to give us a series of lectures on the handling of small arms, particularly revolver and pistol shooting. His lectures were enthralling. He seemed to have the ability to rivet the attention simply by making his lectures damned interesting.

Grant-Taylor had a building set up in England used for constant practise until some nine targets could be hit in a matter of seconds. He duplicated this form of training in other countries of the world where he was invited to pass on his expertise. Quite a character.

Another was Eric Cooper, a captain in the Royal Artillery, which was part of the 1st Indian LAA Regiment. Captain Cooper remembers, 'His name was Grant-Taylor and I went with a number of other officers to a lecture he was giving one afternoon in Central Burma.' The training took place in an aircraft hangar with some staging being turned into a makeshift execution shed. On display was Grant-Taylor's usual paraphernalia of targets, tin cans, sandbags and model figures to conduct his CQB lecture, and then in walked the man himself.

Captain Cooper recalls,

Grant-Taylor strode in through the audience decked in an array of revolvers (large and small) all tucked in his belt. He introduced himself and said he was an American Police Marksman who had been drafted into the Army to show people like us how to be efficient ruthless pistol shooters. In his words how to shoot people without showing fear, pity or remorse! He spoke in short sentences occasionally drawing a gun or two and shooting a target or making a model figure jump across the stage while he moved about.

Corporal Thomas Bell, who served with 44 Commando in Burma, recounts some words of wisdom from Grant-Taylor about the stopping power of large calibre rounds when he was instructing Bell's unit. 'If I could I'd strap a 25-pounder to my belt I would' proclaimed Grant-

Taylor, and 'try to get as big a calibre as you can—if you hit him with a .45, he'll be dead, he'll go down and stay down.'

This was followed by Grant-Taylor himself demonstrating his six-shot card trick with his .45 Colt semi-automatic to the assembled commandos. Not that Grant-Taylor's training lectures were confined to just the humble foot soldier or officer. As he had been in Palestine, he was courted by the military hierarchy in South East Asia who wanted to witness first-hand the training officer who had so inspired a wide body of men. They also wanted to inspect his reputed skills with a pistol. And so it was that on 17 December 1944 Lieutenant-Colonel Grant-Taylor was asked to give a demonstration as part of a passing out class for soldiers and officers that had just completed his five day CQB course for future instructors. The guests of honour at this demonstration, were the Supreme Allied Commander South East Asia Command, Admiral Lord Louis Mountbatten, and his recently appointed Chief of Staff, Lieutenant-General Frederick 'Boy' Browning, the former Commander of the 1st British Airborne Corps.

Of Grant-Taylor, Mountbatten later stated that,

> He is a most extraordinary man, who looks like a rather prosperous country parson, but in fact is probably the greatest British gunman [who is] bringing a new technique and enthusiasm to our troops for killing men at ranges from 15 yards and less, with revolver, automatic and sub-machine gun.

After witnessing Grant-Taylor's lecture, Mountbatten was treated to a display of the gunmen going through the now infamous 'execution shed,' with the future instructors having to complete the usual six-target drill. On this particular occasion, Mountbatten and Browning had witnessed a Ghurkha soldier shoot down all six targets, four of them through the bull's-eye, in less than seven seconds after entering the CQB room. Apparently the day previous, a soldier had done it a second faster.

It was also during this period that a young lieutenant in the 6th Ghurkha Rifles by the name of John Slim, attended one of Grant-Taylor's courses in Nasik, India. As we shall see later, what was seen as a standard course for a young officer to attend in 1945 would have far reaching consequences for the development of CQB training after the war as well as the elite of the British Military Special Forces.

One of his SEAC students remembers Colonel Grant-Taylor thus: 'He was jovial, well liked and admired as a teacher.' As usual Grant-Taylor would make his thoughts known on the subject matter of CQB with his usual bombastic style. 'He would get our attention, and he used to drum into us to have a level of focus on the serious business of killing. The work was hard and rough.'

Several of Grant-Taylor's, by now familiar, catchphrases provided motivational and tactical encouragement for the fledgling gunmen. 'Don't rush the draw—go in a slow hurry! That way you'll be faster,' was for those students unlucky enough to fumble a quick draw, and as for those who were squeamish about killing, he would rumble that 'CQB shooting was to be done without pity, without fear and without remorse'. For those trainee gunmen that tried to teach the expert to suck eggs, there was a short sharp shock in store. At a training camp in Nasik there was a junior officer that was very proud of his small .25 semi-automatic pistol and would frequently try to extol its virtues to Grant-Taylor. Grant-Taylor merely inspected it and tossed it back to the officer with a dismissive 'It's only good for a lady's purse or for when you're on the lavatory!' Grant-Taylor was, as we know, always an advocate of a big calibre to put the enemy down and would have viewed such a pop-gun weapon as a mere toy.

Of the colonel's qualities as an instructor in SEAC and CBI it could in no way be classed as a Wild West show, despite Grant-Taylor's rhetoric to fire up the young soldiers, but instead it was a focused and disciplined lesson on the intricacies of pistol shooting. He would hammer it home by stating that they should 'rehearse, rehearse, and rehearse as much as you can before going on operations.' And for those that doubted Grant-Taylor's natural shooting ability, men who worked with him during this period have stated that in all the time that they worked with him they only ever saw him miss the target once, which is an enviable miss rate for any expert.

Off-duty, which was not often, Grant-Taylor, was disciplined about his drinking and it is on record that he would never turn up for duty inebriated or the worse for wear. Of his past, he was characteristically discreet and non-committal, keeping his cards close to his chest and instead relying on the often inaccurate rumour mill to fill in the blanks about who he was and were he had come from.

What does seem strange about Grant-Taylor's time in CBI was that he was never used by his old mob, SOE. Here he was, active and fully operational in the region, a well known and respected officer capable of delivering his lessons to a wide range of soldiers of all rank, age and experience. From 1944, SOE in South Asia had worked under the cover name Force 136. Its task was to encourage and supply resistance movements across Burma, China, Malaya, India and Thailand. It was also active in more conventional military-style operations behind Japanese lines. So what could be the reason for the exclusion of this talented CQB specialist?

Perhaps he was too much sought after by the mainstream military and was kept within the army's fiefdom by senior officers? Maybe he had stepped on too many toes further up the SOE chain of command, especially in light of the Stormy Petrel accusation during his time in Palestine, and had become blackballed by senior officers. But he would surely have been an asset to the irregular Forces of SOE in Asia. In truth it could have been any or all of the above reasons.

However by 1945, SOE, Force 136, in South East Asia was less concerned with conducting combat operations and was geared more towards the use of sabotage and intelligence gathering. By the time that Grant-Taylor had reached their theatre of operations in 1945, most of the Force 136 personnel were already battle-hardened veterans that were fully experienced in CQB. What is known is that many of the Force 136 Soldiers had been drawn from the regular army and it is quite likely that many had already been through Grant-Taylor's training with their parent regiments at some point in the past.

So was Grant-Taylor's method relevant to this new theatre of war, the new territories in jungles, forests, hills and bunkers? The reasoning for the need for this type of combat was that the men in SEAC-CBI theatre may have to fight in a variety of challenging environments, from jungles, to forests, to towns, as well as a resilient and battle hardened army on their way to the ultimate goal of taking Japan. As such, the men fighting were required to have training in the very latest and very best forms of close quarter battle to deal with these tactical scenarios.

Certainly it had its place in these combat environments, and there are many accounts of the soldier's active in SEAC-CBI using this close quarter method in enemy engagements. The most obvious advantage of Grant-Taylor's method was that a CQB instructor could take a man with no, or limited firearms experience, and was able to successfully teach him to use it in a relatively short period of time. The range in most of these

1. The last photograph taken of Hector Grant-Taylor, *c.* 1950. (*Joss O'Kelly*)

Above & left: 2. & 3. Grant-Taylor's grave in the Quetta cemetery. (*Sue Farrington*)

Below: 4. Portrait of Wilhelmina 'Sophie' Rix taken when she was a teenager. (*Chris Claessens*)

Opposite: 5. Minnie Abbott, the first wife of Hector Grant-Taylor, taken in the 1920s. (*Liz Abbott*)

6. Fort Spin Boldak where Grant-Taylor's Regiment took part in a concerted attack during the 3rd Afghan War. (*Steve Southerland*)

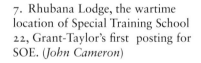

Rhubana Lodge

7. Rhubana Lodge, the wartime location of Special Training School 22, Grant-Taylor's first posting for SOE. (*John Cameron*)

8. Inverailort Castle, Lochailort, Scotland, the wartime home of the commando instructors and Fairbairn and Sykes' 'Silent Killing' training. (*Geoff Murray and Jack Backer*)

9. Major Keith O'Kelly outside the Quetta CQB building. (*Joss O'Kelly*)

10. The Violette Szabo Memorial located on the South Bank of the River Thames in London. A dignified memorial to all the SOE personnel who gave so much.

Above: 11. Sultan, Grant-Taylor and O'Kelly on operations in Quetta. (*Joss O'Kelly*)

Left: 12. The three CQB comrades of the Quetta School. O'Kelly, Grant-Taylor and Sultan Mohammed Khan. (*Joss O'Kelly*)

Opposite above: 13. Grant-Taylor instructing Major-General D. F. McConnell in the correct handling method of the 'Chicago Piano', AKA the Tommy gun, in Palestine *c*.1943. (*Imperial War Museum*)

Opposite below: 14. Grant-Taylor instructing Major-General D. F. McConnell in the fighting crouch position. (*Imperial War Museum*)

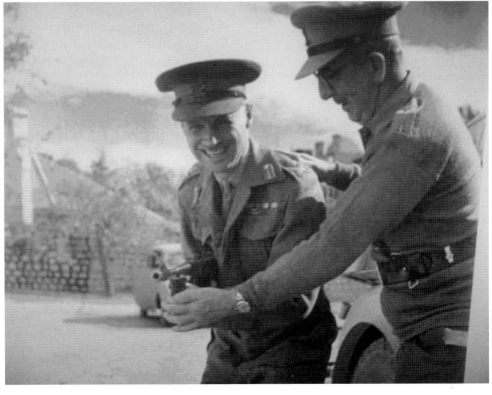

15. & 16. Captain Eric Anthony Sykes, SOE's Silent Killing instructor. (*National Archives*)

Right: 17. Captain Georges Bergé, the French SAS Officer in command of Operation Savanna and Grant-Taylor's inspiration for his alter ego, The Major.

Below: 18. Montagu Grant Wilkinson. Was he the officer that talent-spotted Grant-Taylor for SOE? (*National Portrait Gallery*)

Opposite above: 19. A .38 Calibre Smith & Wesson Model 10, similar to Grant-Taylor's Silver Lady.

Opposite below: 20. British Commando using the Tommy Gun. Grant-Taylor would later nickname it the Chicago Piano!

Above: 21. Proper grip and effective trigger action are imperative for CQB – here a demonstration of Grant-Taylor's 'squeezing the orange' principle. (*Author's collection*)

22. Modern CQB now integrates simunition and unarmed combat into its training syllabus. (*Author's collection*)

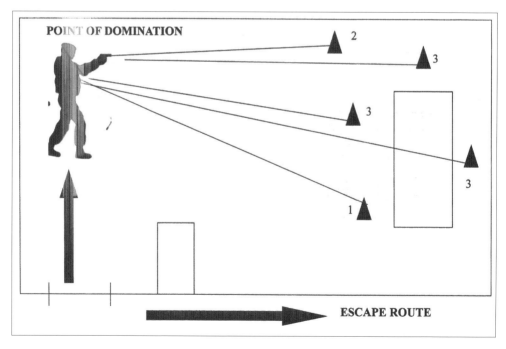

23. Example of a Grant-Taylor Room Combat Assault plan. Note the gunman's 'Point of Domination' where he can fire into multiple targets and the 1, 2, 3 CQB system. (*Modern Combatives Group*)

24. Hostage Rescue Team (HRT) conducting CQB Team Tactics. Many of the methods still in use today can be traced back to the SAS CRW of the 1960s and Grant-Taylor's method of DOMINATING the room. (*Photo courtesy of Squadease*)

Left: 25. CQB practitioners conducting point shooting training.

Below: 26. Modern CQB operators using instinctive 'Quick-Fire' shooting as part of VIP Protection training at a firearms range. (*Author's collection*)

27. Modern combative operator in the F&S/Grant-Taylor fighting crouch. Note the off hand ready to manipulate, defend or strike! (*Author's collection*)

28. SAS Counter Revolutionary Warfare. The culmination of Grant-Taylor's influence on the evolution of Close Quarter Battle (CQB) for the postwar Special Forces. (*Polease and Squadease*)

situations was between three and fifteen feet, and this is where close range point shooting methods excel. We also cannot doubt that Grant-Taylor's natural shooting ability played a part and was a fundamental success to his role as an instructor.

It should be remembered that Grant-Taylor had been practising on a near enough daily basis for almost four years, so his skill level was constantly being improved and honed. Nevertheless, students would see him whip out and blast away, consistently hitting his targets with pin-point accuracy, and could not fail to be impressed and inspired by the man that Mountbatten had referred to as 'the greatest British gunman.'

With the end to the war in Europe fast approaching, life was slowly struggling to return to its pre-1939 normality back in Great Britain. With victory over its enemy and the promise of peace assured, there was still the very real hardship of postwar austerity for the common man to deal with. Hard work was needed to rebuild a war-ravaged nation.

For Sophie Grant-Taylor at home in Surrey things were no less difficult. Her war years had been a constant struggle to make ends meet, and with very little correspondence from Grant-Taylor, aside from the last letter in 1943. It is little wonder, the inevitable happened and she fell in love with someone else.

Having been on virtually full-time active service, with few breaks, it was inevitable that Grant-Taylor's married life would suffer. In truth the pair had been drifting apart for some years before the outbreak of war, and the enforced separation had only heightened the feeling of two people heading off along different paths. Sophie, now in her mid thirties, had started a relationship with a neighbour, William Hicks, a local electrician, and in February 1945 she gave birth to a son, Anthony John, at the family home in Surrey. Obviously, because Grant-Taylor was stationed overseas during this time the boy could not have been his.

This was a not uncommon occurrence in wartime, with families split and never sure if the husband or father of the family would ever be coming home, the attention of both parties could wander, and yet despite all this, it appears that Grant-Taylor and his wife never divorced. This may have been partly due to the fact that Sophie Grant-Taylor did not actually know where in the world her husband was at that time. The last letter that she had received from him had been sent from the Middle East, and she had no idea where he was now.

For propriety's sake, Sophie Grant-Taylor would keep her married name with the boy taking the name of his legitimate father, Hicks. However, looming in the background was the worry of whether Hector Grant-Taylor would re-appear to wreck their domestic bliss. With this hanging over the family, Sophie made the bold decision to pen a letter informing Grant-Taylor of her new son and her long-term intentions for herself, William and Anthony. She posted the letter, hoping that it would reach her estranged husband in time and settled back to start, hesitantly, a new life. The family appears to have been very happy and lived a contented life. Many years later in the summer of 1952, when all the necessary legal requirements had been fulfilled, Sophie would go on to marry William John Hicks at a quiet family service in Surrey.

Seven thousand miles away, Grant-Taylor finally received word from home. The letter had apparently been posted and then passed around the various units where the military thought he could be, before several weeks later finally reaching him in India. It was to be the ubiquitous 'Dear John' correspondence. So when the letter came from home stating that Sophie no longer wanted him in her life, the news was not totally devastating to him. In truth he no longer wished to return to Britain to face the prospect of a loveless marriage, the inevitable divorce proceedings (again), the re-building of his life financially, the unemployment, the rations, the cold and wet weather. Here in Asia he had achieved things beyond his wildest ambitions, had started new relationships, and was finally living the lifestyle that he had coveted for so very, very long. He was respected, admired by his men, rich, affluent and not without influence in certain quarters. He was happy.

He had started his wartime service as a mere private, and here he was, four years later a lieutenant-colonel assigned to secret operations. There was no conceivable way he was going to go back to the drudgery, boredom and the horror of being a non-person again. He immediately went on the offensive and petitioned his senior officers requesting that his demob papers be deferred for as long as possible. So while the majority of the troops were eager to have their demob papers as soon as they could so as to return home, Grant-Taylor was determined to stay in the military.

With the end of hostilities and active operations being wound down, the need for Grant-Taylor's specialist CQB skills were on the wane. The military would need a reason to keep this much-respected senior officer on staff. Where would he fit in? What role would he be able to play as the army was hurrying towards peacetime?

Grant-Taylor's petition appears to have worked as by July of 1946 he was held back, and posted as a class A instructor to a number of military training schools in India. Whilst still retaining his rank of Lieutenant-Colonel, Grant-Taylor was, on the surface, about to spend the remainder of his military career being shifted around the various training centres in the region running basic training programmes for new officer recruits.

For a CQB specialist this must have been very much like a racehorse pulling a cart, and the prospect of it undoubtedly frustrated him to a greater degree. Unfortunately it was the price he was forced to accept in order to remain in the British Army. But, as with most things in his life, he appears to have been in the right place at the right time once again, for while the Nazi and Japanese threat had been well and truly eliminated, there was a new conflict growing in Asia that would require all the lethal skills that he spent so long perfecting.

CHAPTER SEVEN:

The Quetta CQB School: Endgame

1946–1950

My life is simple, my food is plain, and my quarters are uncluttered.
In all things, I have sought clarity. I face the troubles and problems of
life and death willingly. Virtue, integrity and courage are my priorities.
I can be approached, but never pushed; befriended but never coerced;
killed but never shamed.

Yi Sunshin, Korean Naval Commander (1545–1598)

By late 1946 Grant-Taylor had chosen to remain in the Army on the
active service list for the next three years and on the reserve list for the
next five years. After initially being tasked to work as a staff instructor at
the regional military staff colleges in India, Grant-Taylor's wartime skills
were once again to be used to train a new generation of combatants
belonging to the Indian Army.

There was a wave of political and postwar colonial restructuring
going on, with borders being re-drawn, new countries being formed and
by 1947, British officers of the Indian Army who were stationed in the
Northern Frontier would suddenly find themselves in a newly formed
country, Pakistan.

Now stationed in Rawalpindi, Grant-Taylor had been asked to set up
a security unit and conduct his CQB training programme for Pakistani
Army personnel and their British officers. This mission arrived at just
the right time for Grant-Taylor. He had been slowly getting bored at
the prospect of staff colleges and boredom was leading to drinking both
heavily and frequently to while away the days. It was a cycle that he

knew had to stop, not only for his career but for his health also. He was now nearing sixty years of age and the lifestyle that he had been leading over the past eight years was beginning to take its toll on his health.

So when the mission to Rawalpindi landed in his lap, he jumped at the chance with enthusiasm to dust off his old shooting skills and get back into the great game, where he was happiest. The CQB training was to take place at Pakistan's main army garrison and military centre just outside Rawalpindi and was set up along similar lines as his previous wartime lectures with a wide range of military units and officers being inducted into the training. The techniques and teaching methods remained, as it had done during the wartime years, with the overall emphasis being on attack, attack, and attack at close range.

One of the attendees on this course was a young captain in the Armoured Corps, by the name of Keith O'Kelly. O'Kelly had been born in India during the early part of the century and joined the British Indian Army as an officer with the Armoured Corps. He had been one of the first students at Grant-Taylor's CQB programme at the base in Rawalpindi, and in Grant-Taylor's own words, 'he displayed keenness and enthusiasm to such an extent that on the conclusion of the course I sought him as an assistant instructor whenever he could be spared from his own unit—he is an outstanding performer with the revolver, automatic pistol and sub machine carbine.'

Captain O'Kelly evidently had found his forte, as Grant-Taylor later trusted him enough to take command of several future training modules and he had also represented the Northern Command in numerous pistol team shooting matches with consistent results.

O'Kelly had also been involved with Grant-Taylor in the evacuation by road of British civilians from Kashmir prior to the outbreak of hostilities. In October of that year, the Kashmir situation was reaching boiling point and Pathan tribesmen from the frontier were encouraged by the Pakistan authorities to invade and oppose Indian Army troops who flew into the Vale of Kashmir from the South.

As Major O'Kelly later recalled in an article published in 1998:

Amid all this turmoil, another serious emergency became apparent—the safe evacuation of British residents from Kashmir. Many of these were retired Indian army officers, government officials and their families, who had decided to spend their declining years in this beautiful state. Some were in houseboats on Dal Lake, others in bungalows in the environs of Srinagar, and a few in the idyllic surroundings of Gulmarg and Pahlgarm.

Now their plans for a peaceful retirement were instantly shattered, and they were facing an extremely precarious situation. A few had already been massacred and their possessions looted by Pathan tribesmen. These latter were not terribly interested in the political situation or establishing Pakistan's right to the State of Kashmir. As was their heritage, many were bent on loot and plunder, and quickly returned to their tribal homelands.

Under the command of Brigadier Ian Lauder of the 7th Division, and with Colonel Grant-Taylor as Second in Command of the rescue operation, Captain O'Kelly and his men brought up the rear of the evacuation with an armoured convoy.

This young officer had obviously impressed Grant-Taylor during this operation. He was tall, fit, tough, and daring, everything that a modern British Army officer should be, and in a later memorandum, he said of O'Kelly, 'it is my considered view that the successful outcome of the convoy with all personnel and vehicles intact is in large measure due to the speedy work put in by the L.A.D. on the dangerous road from Srinagar to Rawalpindi.'

The captain and the colonel soon became fast friends. Major O'Kelly remembers Grant-Taylor being 'quiet and secretive about his previous activities—as you would expect. He was always very reticent about his past.'

As for their social life, there was always the Officers' Club Bar where bonds and friendships could be formed. But of Grant-Taylor, Major O'Kelly recalls, respectfully, details of him being a, 'hard drinker but in many years I never saw him inebriated at work or during lectures. He could take it!'

So it was with much sadness, that in January 1948, Keith O'Kelly asked to be posted to England. Captain O'Kelly had been offered a promotion to stay in Pakistan, but partly due to domestic reasons (his close family had recently returned to England due to the volatile political situation in the region) and wanting to be with them, he chose this time to move on. By the end of 1947 Grant-Taylor, still riding high from his successful CQB training mission in Rawalpindi, was asked to take on the position of the Commandant of the Corps of the Pakistan Military Police Centre (CPMP) in nearby Abbotabad.

The CPMP was formed by the British Royal Military Police in 1946 and it was initially the part of the Corps of Military Police of the Indian Army. With the independence of Pakistan in 1947, the military police was established shortly afterwards, when elements of active duty corps of military police arrived at Abbottabad Military District (AMC).

Pakistan at this time was perhaps one of the most dangerous places on the planet, and thousands of refugees on the India–Pakistan border were murdered. The British attempted to be neutral to both races, Muslim and Hindu, and assist them in going to their new homelands. Pakistan at this time was still a Commonwealth protectorate, and as such the crown had a number of responsibilities, namely providing a professionally trained police and military force, run along British Army lines.

Grant-Taylor's remit was to be a new broom to organise this academy, create an effective training syllabus, and form four military police units for various regional areas. On a day-to-day basis, the CPMP's role would be law enforcement within the Pakistan army, which would include misconduct and criminal investigations. In times of war they would also be called upon to handle PoWs.

With the advent of numerous border disputes and low-intensity conflicts in the region, the CPMP units would be at the forefront of the fighting, and therefore they needed to be one of the elite units of the Pakistan army. This would be reflected in the specialist training that they were given.

However for Colonel Grant-Taylor, the position of commandant seems to have been only a temporary one, as by the end of his first year he was offered another mission, once again, of setting up a new Close Quarter Battle School over a 1,000 kilometres away in the west of Pakistan, close to the Afghanistan border.

The city of Quetta is situated at an average elevation of 1,680 metres (5,500 feet) above sea level, making it Pakistan's only high-altitude, major city, and consists of series of valleys which act as a natural fort, surrounded on all sides by hills named Chiltan, Takatoo, Murdar and Zarghun. Quetta derives its name from the Pashto word *kuwatta*, which means a fort.

In February 1949, the military police expanded by establishing a CQB School in Quetta to impart training to officers, NCOs and soldiers from the Corps of Military Police and other specialist Indian Army regiments.

In late 1948, Major Keith O'Kelly returned to Pakistan to take up a position with his former mentor Colonel Grant-Taylor. He had an interesting assignment for his young protégé, and he wanted the best people he could for this prestigious operation. Grant-Taylor had recently extended his service with the military for an extra three years, and recognising that his career would be coming to an end in the near future, was determined to go out doing what he excelled at and what he enjoyed.

Like a postwar Fairbairn and Sykes, they were to establish a close quarter battle school at the Quetta Military Staff College. The school would consist of a number of firing ranges, armoury, a killing house as well as an assault course and gymnasium. Under Grant-Taylor's tutelage, the Quetta CQB School was set up along similar lines to the wartime training programmes that the colonel had run in Palestine and Europe, with unarmed, pistol and sub-machine gun lessons. The exception being that in this theatre of operations greater emphasis was placed on the close quarter shooting aspects than the unarmed combat.

There was a severe training regime to bring the indigenous troops up to an acceptable level of fitness, with Grant-Taylor constantly hammering out his now infamous motivational slogans —'Murder is my business' and 'There are only two types of gunmen: the quick and the dead.'

Once again this type of gung-ho rhetoric could be seen as mere hyperbole on the part of the instructor. But underneath, it has a very real point to offer. Grant-Taylor was teaching these men how to kill at close quarters, quite often in very cramped conditions where the enemy is a mere few feet away, close enough that you can literally see the whites of his eyes. To unhesitatingly enter a room, and gun a man down is not something for the faint hearted, and can have potentially tragic consequences if the gunman hesitates or allows his conscience to take over.

It has always been the opinion that the actual physical motion of killing, especially with a firearm, is the easy part—aim, pull the trigger and bang! But the real problem lies with allowing the mind to take control and introduce both doubts over what you are doing, and having the individual's conscience to run wild. Even for a soldier tasked to kill his enemy it can, in certain situations, be a difficult thing to live with. After all soldiers are created, not born.

Therefore, the war-hungry fighting talk is necessary to fire up the trainee and the terminology used such as 'Hun,' 'Jerry' or 'Jap' is introduced to dehumanise the enemy and see them as nothing more than faceless, nameless sacks of meat walking around waiting to be blown apart by large calibre bullets. This method is not fool-proof, far from it, but as an extension to the physical weapons training, this mental 'toughening up' was, for its day, ground-breaking.

Joining Grant-Taylor and O'Kelly on the training staff was another young officer, Captain Sultan Mohammed Khan. Sultan Mohammed Khan, after graduating from Islamia College Lahore, Punjab University, had joined the British Indian Army in 1941, and was later commissioned as an officer in 1942 with the 5th Baloch, (Jacob Rifles). An all round sportsman who had during his university days been a prolific athlete, coupled with a fine brain and a dry wit made him a shining example of the modern day Indian Army officer. He later joined the Frontier Force regiment in 1948, which is where he came to the attention of Grant-Taylor and O'Kelly. It was this trilogy of CQB specialists that eventually went on to shape the running and ethos of the Quetta CQB School and introduce the small arms training that had had its baptism of fire during the conflicts in Europe, Asia and the Middle East.

When he had first arrived in India in 1946 Grant-Taylor had brought with him a new wife, Mel Grant-Taylor. The pair had swept into the region like a latter-day maharaja and his lady and had soon set tongues wagging. Mel was actually the nickname of Kathleen Melita Laborde. Born in 1901, Kathleen was the middle daughter in a family of five siblings of Maximus Horace Laborde, a retired Royal Naval officer, and Margaret Laborde. The well-to-do Labordes had an elegant residence in London and a lifestyle to match as befitted the family of a Royal Naval Commander.

Kathleen would later go on to gain qualifications as a physiotherapist and bio-physical assistant Masseuse from the Society of Apothecaries of London, while working, amongst others, at Carshalton Children's hospital, Surrey. From the mid-1930s onwards she seems to have developed her father's love of adventure and travelled to Egypt in 1936, working as part of the local British Embassy as a pensions assistant and secretary, before returning to Britain in 1938.

The pair had initially met in Egypt in 1944 when Kathleen appears to have been attached to the local consulate with rumours that she worked as part of the backroom staff at the SIS Cairo Station. Grant-Taylor, as we know, used this as his base of operations between travelling around on various training assignments in the region, and it was not uncommon for two people sharing the 'secret world' to become intimately involved in this manner.

The couple's relationship seems to have started as a casual thing, but was sustained over a number of years while Grant-Taylor was away in various parts of the Middle East, Italy and CBI. However with the end of his marriage from Sophie in 1945, Grant-Taylor had made a move to take Kathleen with him to India and to legitimise their relationship on a more permanent basis.

How much Grant-Taylor had told his new wife about his already existing marital status is open to question. For example, was Kathleen aware that he was already married back in England? Was she still quite content to live the life of an officer's wife assured in the knowledge that they were neither keen to return back to the UK to face any consequences? Or was she blissfully unaware of his previous life and convinced that she was his one and only wife? Had they indeed married, or was it merely Kathleen adopting the surname Grant-Taylor so that they could live together as man and wife without scrutiny from the at times prudish expatriate community?

This was not unusual among the British soldiers stationed in India and Pakistan. Many would 'marry' local or European women that had made a new life in Asia, quite often with the marriage certificate being nothing more than a brief note written on a scrap of paper by the soldiers themselves with no legal basis whatsoever. Some of these soldiers seemed to regard these marriages as temporary, and it was only when they were recalled back to the UK that the relationship ended and problems arose. Whatever the actual truth, from 1947 onwards, Kathleen Melita Laborde would consistently go by the name Kathleen 'Mel' Grant-Taylor up until the day she died.

In Pakistan the couple set up home at a bungalow on one of the main roads leading into Quetta, complete with house servants, and happily integrated themselves into the local military community. The expatriate community of Quetta, encompassing the military personnel and their families, all lived in or near the staff college itself or at the Chiltan Hotel in small apartments with them all sharing a communal dining room and facilities. This included the conveniently located Quetta Officers' Club where officers could relax and enjoy a drink. Sports facilities consisted of a swimming pool and tennis courts.

On the whole Quetta, for the small British military presence and their families, was quite a comfortable posting, with many viewing it in the immediate postwar years as a good career stepping stone with the added advantage of it being a more luxurious lifestyle than was seen in some of the more desperate colonial outposts. And while the winters could be harsh and cruel at times, there was still enough of a social and sporting life during the fine seasons to keep even the most enthusiastic families entertained. With races to the top of Mount Murdar, cross country horse races, gymkhanas, polo, horticultural clubs, swimming and boating on Hanna Lake it was a veritable home away from home. A little England nestled deep in the heart of Asia.

Back at the staff college there would quite often be VIP guests eager to see the workings of the CQB School. The most notable of these was The Shah of Iran, Mohammad Reza Shah Pahlava, who was on a tour of the region in 1948 in order to mend relationships between Pakistan and Iran. The Shah was eager to meet the legendary chief instructor, Colonel Grant-Taylor, and witness at first-hand the shooting prowess that had been represented so vividly by senior officers.

Unfortunately, that morning Grant-Taylor was not up to the task due to being ill, and Major O'Kelly stepped into the breach taking Grant-Taylor's place for the CQB room combat demo. The Shah being keen to get a feel for the action asked if he could go into the CQB room and participate. This sent his personal bodyguards into a flap. They were not to keen to have a member of the Royal Family in the same vicinity as a loaded firearm! The Shah however insisted and went into the CQB room safely behind Major O'Kelly as he eliminated the dummy targets with his usual aplomb.

The demonstration was a great success and the Shah was suitably impressed with the close quarter shooting skills of Grant-Taylor's officers. At a garden party for the officers and their families, the Shah presented an exquisite Persian carpet to be donated to top the officers' mess, and later that day he dined with all from the CQB school and the staff college that were involved with his tour. Several months later the

107

President of Pakistan, Ayub Khan, also visited the CQB School and he too left suitably impressed with the shooting prowess of the elite of the Indian Army.

In early 1950, with the continuing border wars becoming more frequent, Colonel Grant-Taylor was dispatched on a short mission to East Pakistan, prior to the Indian Army's invasion operation. He was only there a matter of weeks, but sometime during that period he started to feel distinctly unwell. This was quite unusual for him as he prided himself on being a tough old boot and having the constitution of a rock. 'I've lived in slit trenches, deserts, swamps and jungles and never caught even a cold,' he once proudly stated of his health. However it seems that this time his luck had run dry. Upon returning to Quetta he was admitted to the Quetta Military Hospital. There he rested while the doctors went to work on him. It did not take them long to discover that he was already in the latter stages of Typhoid fever. Typhoid, when it strikes, can be a long, painful and lethal illness. It is insidious.

Untreated typhoid fever is divided into four individual stages, each lasting approximately one week. In the first week, the temperature rises slowly and a burning hot fever ensues. In the second week the patient lies prostrate and can slip into a state of delirium. The abdomen is distended and painful and diarrhoea can occur in this stage. In the third week a number of complications can occur including intestinal haemorrhaging and perforation, delirium and metastatic abscesses. This can carry on into the fourth and final week.

Typhoid fever in most cases is not fatal. However, in Grant-Taylor's case by the time the doctors had made a successful diagnosis he was already in its final stages and it had taken its toll on him quite severely. He was already very weak and dehydrated and was starting to slip away. Eventually the battle against the disease came to an end, and the once mighty soldier that had fought in two World Wars and inspired a generation of Special Forces warriors, was finally brought low. Colonel Grant-Taylor died on 22 August 1950. His final visitor was his friend and colleague, Major Keith O'Kelly.

Grant-Taylor's burial took place a week later. He was buried at the Military Cemetery on Baleli Road, Quetta. In accordance with his rank of Colonel he was given full military honours, with a full battalion, 600 rifles of the Frontier Force Regiment of the Pakistani Army following the coffin. The service was well attended by, amongst others, Major O'Kelly and a whole host of friends and colleagues from the military mission and staff college.

His gravestone, commissioned by his colleagues, stated simply:

IN MEMORY OF COLONEL GRANT-TAYLOR.
DIED 22nd AUGUST 1950.
ERECTED BY HIS BROTHER MASONS AND OFFICERS

With their friend gone, the question now turned as to what arrangements should be made for his widow. It did not take long to discover that Grant-Taylor and Mel had not actually been married. Instead their relationship was that of a common-law marriage, and despite her taking the Grant-Taylor name, there was no legal basis for her to remain in Quetta.

Arrangements were quickly made for her to be repatriated back to England, and her elder sister Mary Laborde hastily travelling to Quetta to bring her back. The sisters travelled on the steam ship *The Circassia* from Bombay via Karachi, arriving in Liverpool on 25 September 1950.

Following the upheaval of his death, there were several discreet notices and tributes paid to him. Perhaps the most poignant came from the members of the Kipling Society of London, a private group devoted to the works of Rudyard Kipling. His obituary was posted (belatedly) on page ten in the October 1951 edition of the Society Journal and was written by the editor at the time E. D. W. Chaplin.

Colonel H. Grant-Taylor:

It is with regret that we learn, at this late date, of the death of one of our members, Colonel H. Grant-Taylor, around whose career, Kipling, if he still lived, could weave a story of adventure and fun.

Short and plump, with wry face and heavy glasses, Grant-Taylor was a Dickensian character who will be hard to replace. Known throughout the world, he was an expert in the short-range weapons of today.

America knew him when suffering from the gangster menaces of Al Capone and others like him. England knew him when he trained and operated with Commandos in the last war. The Japanese knew him from the results produced by his trained gunmen from India, and his other exploits in Egypt, Palestine and the Caucasus would provide material for a Baroness Orczy thriller!

He died of typhoid in Quetta on August 22nd 1950, as he lived, with a smile and a joke, leaving behind a widow and a host of friends in all corners of the world.

And of the other lady in his life, his constant companion throughout his wartime years, the Silver Lady? What became of her?

Following his death, as is customary in the military, Grant-Taylor's belongings were auctioned off within the military garrison. However, Major-General Lauder (the senior officer in Quetta) ordered that Major O'Kelly should take possession of Grant-Taylor's personal firearms. This included a German Army Luger pistol, a US Army Colt .45 pistol, and of course the Silver Lady. 'He would occasionally exhibit it [the Silver Lady] in a demonstration. But on operations he preferred the US Army Colt .45 automatic pistol for its vicious impact on a recipient,' remembers O'Kelly.

This retention of all of Grant-Taylor's personal weapons did not sit well with O'Kelly and so he made the decision to retain the Colt and the Luger, and to donate the Silver Lady to the CQB School in Quetta in memory of its founder and commanding officer. The Silver Lady remained at the school for many years on display, until the school was eventually demolished to make way for a new building. It was during this period that the revolver disappeared.

The most likely explanation of its whereabouts is that it was taken for 'safe keeping' by a senior officer and passed or sold into private ownership. In later years Major O'Kelly always regretted not taking the third pistol into safe keeping and perhaps saving his friend's talisman.

Leonard Duncan Hector Grant-Taylor was such a *tour de force*, a big personality, a larger-than-life figure that it is sometimes easy to forget that his story is as much about the people and situations that he moved around during his life as it was about the man himself. He was the sun to their satellite planets. And of the supporting characters in this story, what became of them?

Following Grant-Taylor's death, Major Keith O'Kelly stayed in Quetta at the CQB School less than twelve months. He no longer wished to serve under anyone else's command and in 1951 returned to the UK where he subsequently joined the Parachute Regiment and had a successful career.

Sultan continued to serve in the Pakistan Army for many years, eventually attaining the rank of Lieutenant-Colonel. Following his retirement from the military he would later go on to serve in a number of government positions and would often be called upon to organise hunting expeditions for dignitaries such as the President of Pakistan and Prince Phillip, the Duke of Edinburgh. 'Uncle' Sultan is now happily retired, still living in Quetta, and surrounded by his loving family who happily dote upon him.

Following Major O'Kelly's departure, the Quetta CQB School came under the command of Major James Arthur Colquhoun, a thirty-five-year-old officer, serving in the Indian Army. Major Colquhoun carried on Grant-Taylor's tradition and ethos of CQB training until he left the Quetta post in 1955 when he was transferred to serve as a military advisor in Aden.

When news finally reached her of her husband's death, Sophie Grant-Taylor began the legal process of becoming a widow, for which she needed proof of Grant-Taylor's death and sent off for a copy of his death certificate. Curiously when Grant-Taylor's death certificate finally arrived it had a mysterious inconsistency in it: his name was registered as Lionel Hector Grant-Taylor. Sophie subsequently married William Hicks in Surrey in 1952. Three years later, Sophie Hicks, as Grant-Taylor's last legal wife, eventually received a sum of money from his will. He left her, the not inconsiderable amount for the 1950s, of £123, 11s 4d.

Kathleen 'Mel' Grant-Taylor returned to England in 1950 where she resided for much of her life with her sister Mary at their address in the Royal Borough of Kensington, London. She returned to work as a clerical officer in the Foreign and Commonwealth Office in Whitehall. Kathleen retained the Grant-Taylor name, meaning that at one point in the early 1950s there were two widows calling themselves Mrs Grant-Taylor living in England. One wonders if through some rhyme or reason they became aware of each other?

Kathleen Melita Grant-Taylor passed away in September of 1969 aged sixty-eight. Her death certificate states that she had been 'the widow of Alastair Grant-Taylor MC, a Lieutenant-Colonel (Special Services).' Again, another twist in a tale already filled with blurred truth. And that is where Grant-Taylor's story would have ended, as another soldier buried in a foreign field, who would in time, be forgotten about.

However in 2010, a further twist was to occur in this already remarkable story. Uncle Sultan, now in his dotage, and his family decided to pay a visit to the cemetery on Baleli Road and search for the graves of several old comrades from his military days. After much searching they discovered that Grant-Taylor's grave was missing.

The end to this tale is even more tragic and was only discovered later through local press reports. In November 2001, with more civil unrest rife in the region from neighbouring Afghanistan, an armed gang of pro-Taliban extremists attacked the Baleli Road Cemetery in Quetta. They viciously attacked the grounds caretaker, seventy-eight year-old Rasoul Bakhush, hospitalised his son and kidnapped his daughter-in-law. A month earlier, Mr Bakhush had been forced to hide inside his house when demonstrators broke into the cemetery after Friday prayers and demolished several of the colonial graves. One of these was the gravestone of Colonel Grant-Taylor.

According to reports Mr Bakhush had tried his best to continue his work by trying to repair the damage to the graves of some fifteen British soldiers after the pro-Taliban demonstration on 8 October 2001. Smashed crosses have been cemented together and paint splashed over the tombs has been washed off.

'I wanted to repair the damage done because my family has always worked for the British. We were looked after under their rule and it made me sad to see these gravestones broken, so I did my best with what I had to put it right,' he is quoted as saying.

Over the following years with no one to tend, repair or replace them, the graves became overgrown and dilapidated, and for several the damage was just too severe, resulting in them being removed.

And so the man known for more than half his life as Leonard Duncan Hector Grant-Taylor, died as he lived, surrounded by controversy, mystery and intrigue.

CHAPTER EIGHT

Special Forces:
The Grant-Taylor Lineage

1957–2012

Evolution: A gradual process in which something changes into a different and usually more complex or better form.

WITHOUT FEAR—WITHOUT PITY—WITHOUT REMORSE
Colonel Grant-Taylor's CQB Motto, 1945

Following the end of the Second World War there was, perhaps rather understandably, a reluctance to continue the training methods of close quarter combat for the regular army. The nation had had enough of the bloodshed and violence of the past five years and specialist units such as SOE and other irregular forces were either disbanded or its personnel were pooled into regular units.

After the war, the world had moved on, and with the emergence of the Cold War and nuclear warfare, the attention had shifted from regional conflicts to a more global threat. The orthodox, it now seems, had little time for the unorthodox and the men who had been special forces, undercover agents and covert operators returned home to their families and peacetime occupations. For the most part the time of the irregular warrior was over.

However, a consequence of the Second World War was the receding of some old tensions across Palestine, India and Pakistan in order to fight the Axis powers. But with the Nazi defeat, in some cases, came the return to pick up arms and fight old wars with grudges that needed to be settled and resolved, many of them in colonies of the British Empire.

Battles were fought, and here there was a place for the irregular soldier and covert operator.

While Colonel Grant-Taylor continued to ply his trade in India and Pakistan in the late 1940s, in his old stomping ground of Palestine there was a dirty undercover war in progress that consisted of terror gangs and counter-terror gangs. Many of the operators that were dealing with numerous counter-terrorist operations had previously been students of Grant-Taylor's during the war and, as would be expected, many of the operations were usually conducted in an environment that was conducive to Grant-Taylor's CQB technique.

Following his lectures in 1943, the Palestine Police Force had kept his CQB method in place as the standard course for firearms training, and this was later endorsed for the mobile and Special Squads by another former student of Grant-Taylor's—Roy Farran.

In 1947, Farran had been drafted in to operate in Palestine where he was to take the fight to Jewish terrorist organisations such as the Irgun and the Stern gang. This was at a time when the Jewish resistance groups were conducting a violent terrorist war against the British Forces stationed there. One of the turning points in this war was the bombing of the King David Hotel in 1946, which was the main base of the British administration and army HQ in Jerusalem. Secreted somewhere in its offices was also the anti-terrorist section of the Palestine Police Force. Seven milk churns packed with high explosives were placed under the south wing of the hotel and detonated without warning, killing 91 and leaving 110 people injured.

In response, the then Inspector General of the PPF, Nicol Gray, had authorised the creation of a number of special units to assist the police in dealing with this ever growing threat. The PPF had initially created a mobile force, consisting of 800 soldiers who had seen action in North Africa, Italy and the Mediterranean. Their aim was to be a mobile paramilitary quick reaction force against both Jewish and Arab extremist groups. Palestine at this time was essentially a war within a war and both sides had reasoned that it was time to take the gloves off and to start fighting dirty. This was further supplemented by a specialist unit that was to take the fight directly to the terrorists and apply pre-emptive strikes as and when required. Operating under the control of Brigadier Bernard Ferguson, a former Chindit under Orde-Wingate, a special unit was formed that was to be split into two geographical areas.

One team would operate in Haifa to the North under the command of Alastair Macgregor a former SAS soldier, while Farran's team would be based in Jerusalem and the surrounding areas to the south.

Recruitment to this special squad was largely confined to those with counter-intelligence and special operations experience, something that the Palestine police were keen to capitalise on, and many of the new recruits came fresh from the wartime SOE, SIS and the special forces. These special squads would track and hunt down Jewish terrorist operatives in the backstreets and warrens of Palestine in what was to be a bloody and brutal undercover war.

Operator training consisted of short, intensive courses in the Grant-Taylor method of pistol shooting as well as the run through at the *ad hoc* CQB killing house for practising room combat. Once this basic killer training was completed, the officers of Farran's 'Q' (undercover) squads would then infiltrate themselves into the local population and make hard arrests of terrorist insurgents.

Farran and his Q-squads were nothing if not controversial with many in the PPF viewing these special units as an accident waiting to happen, and being a million miles away from the ethos of the mainstream PPF. Then of course there was also Farran himself and his bloody reputation which included being wanted for murder, because he allegedly ordered and took part in the execution of a young Jewish activist, Alexander Rubowitz. Rubowitz's body was never found, presumed buried in a shallow grave somewhere, and Farran subsequently fled to Syria when a criminal investigation was launched against him. He was later court-martialled.

It did not take long for a reprisal attack against Farran. In 1948 after returning home from Palestine, a parcel was sent to the Farran home in Staffordshire. It was marked for the attention of R. Farran. It was subsequently opened, not by Roy Farran who was away at the time, but by his younger brother, Rex. The package is said to have arrived almost one year to the day after Alexander Rubowitz had disappeared. The bomb, which was believed to have been sent by UK-based members of the Stern Gang, exploded, killing Rex Farran instantly.

Following his military service, Roy Farran tried his hand at many things including local politics, writing and teaching. He eventually settled in Alberta, Canada and died from the long-term effects of throat cancer in 2006. In truth, the Q-squads, whilst certainly robust on operations, suffered from having poor intelligence gathering as well as a lack of suitably trained intelligence officers that could speak the language. Eventually in 1948, and with the forthcoming forming of the State of Israel, the special squads, along with much of the Palestine Police Force, was disbanded.

By the early 1950s the last remnants of Grant-Taylor's protégés had come to the end of their respective careers, battles had been fought, won and lost and the need for battle crouches, 'squeezing the orange' and instinctive fire were seen as being obsolete and were soon destined to be eradicated from mainstream military teachings.

The last link from the wartime years, W. E. Fairbairn, was still teaching CQB during the 1950s to both British military units in Cyprus and the Singapore Police Force. His long time training partner Eric Anthony Sykes had died in 1945, with Fairbairn following him fifteen years later. With the passing of these CQB instructors, there was the very real risk that, aside from a few manuals, there would be no one left to pass on these teachings first-hand or that the methods would fade into obscurity. And it would have continued that way until 1957, when a bright young officer with the recently reformed Special Air Service started to search out training methods that he felt could assist the new regiment in its postwar role.

The postwar Special Air Service Regiment had been formed as part of the Territorial Army in 1947, and named the 21st SAS Regiment, (Artists Rifles). Several years later this Territorial Army unit would eventually become absorbed into the Malay Scouts (SAS) which had been set up under the control of Colonel Mike Calvert in response to the Malaya Emergency, and by late 1952 this would see it renamed 22 SAS.

Its remit as a jungle warfare unit, was to search and destroy the Chinese Communist Terrorists (CT) who lived in the deep jungle. Calvert's plan was simple; he would win the hearts and minds of the local population and therefore deny the terrorists food, logistical support and safe havens. At the same time operations would continue to attack known enemy bases and to strive to decimate enemy forces.

John Slim, who had been taught the CQB method personally by Grant-Taylor in India, was one of the early postwar officers recruited into the SAS in 1952. Born in 1927, the son of Field Marshal Viscount Slim, he had been educated at the Prince of Wales's Royal Indian Military

College, Dehra Dun and was commissioned into the Indian Army, just after his eighteenth birthday in July 1945, into the 6th Ghurkha Rifles.

Following the split between the British and Indian armies upon independence, Slim transferred to the British Army and received a commission in the Argyll and Sutherland Highlanders in July 1948. Four years later he joined the Malay Scouts (SAS) as a troop commander.

In the spring of 1956, Slim had been promoted to Major in 22 SAS. A few years later, and now in command of a squadron, he was sent to Kenya, ostensibly for three months to train in African jungle techniques. Slim was also there to trial a new form of CQB to the SAS that he was keen to introduce and to see if these techniques would be useful or even if they could be improved upon.

The training camp was based outside the market town of Nanyuki, in the foothills of Mount Kenya, and consisted of slit trenches dug out of a crater where the troopers would creep along in the battle crouch, pistol at the ready, firing at playing card sized targets stuck to a pole inserted in the ground. The SAS troopers were expected to fire into the playing card at fifteen feet and hit consistently. There was also a rudimentary CQB killing house consisting of sandbagged rooms for advanced training in room combat.

The pistol of choice at that time, was the standard Browning 9 mm. A reliable weapon, that came with a twelve-shot magazine capacity (twelve in the magazine and one ready in the chamber) and was noted for being able to pack a punch. This turned the weapon from being once seen as a purely defensive tool, to an aggressive option for pre-emptively taking the fight to the enemy.

Slim's premise was simple. The regiment needed to adapt for a new type of enemy, an enemy that the SAS would have to engage at close quarters and accept its new role as a leader in these new aspects of modern warfare.

However, after trialling the Grant-Taylor method in Kenya, the collective experience reasoned that, while the Grant-Taylor shooting method was an excellent system to start from, it would definitely need to be updated. Slim put together a small group of senior regiment NCOs who were selected to test out and devise a new training syllabus that would encompass the integration of an unarmed combat system and an update to the existing Grant-Taylor method. The SAS quickly dropped the idea of Grant-Taylor's battle crouch and close-hip firing position, and instead opted for a more upright stance coupled with a shoulder height straight shooting arm.

It was here that these instructors formulated not only the CQB shooting method, but also set the ground rules for the bodyguard training techniques that the SAS would go on to promote throughout the world to the UK's allies.

The CQB training was conducted over an intense two-week period and included dry-fire and live fire range practise with over 1,000 rounds being fired during the course of the programme. It was to grow to be the core of the SAS CQB method. For the unarmed combat portion, the first thing the SAS training group did was look at what had already been used during wartime, and many of the special forces initial unarmed combat methods came straight from the pages of Fairbairn's *All-In Fighting* and Colonel Rex Applegate's *Kill or Get Killed* manual. The new SAS CQB method was soon to have its very own trial by fire in another undercover war that echoed, at least for the soldiers on the ground, that which had taken place in Palestine over a decade earlier.

The seaport city of Aden had always been of strategic value, partly because of its geographical location and partly due to its thriving commercial ports. The British had ruled in Aden as part of British India since 1839 until 1967 when it was known as the Aden Settlement.

On 18 January 1963, the Colony of Aden was absorbed into the Federation of Arab Emirates of the South. This was counter to the political standpoint of the communists of North Yemen who claimed the city and South Yemen as part of their territory. The opening salvo in this territorial dispute, later known as the Aden Emergency, began with a grenade attack by the communist National Liberation Front (NLF), against the British High Commissioner on 10 December 1963. The attack killed one person and injured fifty.

The situation deteriorated even further when rival groups the NLF and FLOSY (Front for the Liberation of Occupied South Yemen) started an almost fratricidal war of attrition, with the rival groups attacking both each other and the British forces. As the NLF and FLOSY groups' confidence grew, so did the frequency and level of ruthlessness of their terror attacks upon the British force. The methods that the terrorists and extremists used involved a variety of ambush tactics, everything from using pregnant women as gun couriers, to lobbing grenades into crowded marketplaces, using children as gunmen to shoot at white men and there were even rumours of professional assassins that had been trained in East Germany, China and Russia.

The *modus operandi* of these professional terrorists was to blindside the intended victim and place the muzzle of the weapon inches from the target head before firing. They would, in the confusion, melt back into the crowded marketplace. These actions could not go unchecked. A response was needed, and as we have previously seen with Farran's Q-squads in Palestine, it was normally the reserve of small independently run special forces teams that would act as a counter-terror force. It was in this crucible that the SAS counter-terrorist teams were to make their mark.

There were two SAS bases in Aden. The first was to the north to cater for the mountain war, with the second HQ base of operations, for the urban counter-terrorist war, based at Ballycastle House, a former RAF married quarter's billet, in Khormaksar. Operating under the codename, Operation NINA, and working out of Ballycastle House, the twenty-man strong counter-terrorist team would go out at various times into the districts of Sheik Othman and Crater, mingling with the locals, blending in disguised in Arab dress. Their primary aim was to gather usable intelligence on suspected extremists, conduct reconnaissance, and on occasion should the opportunity present itself, conduct offensive operations to eliminate with extreme prejudice terrorist targets. Among the SAS itself these undercover operations were unofficially known as 'keeni-meeni' jobs, in reference to the Swahili phrase for the covert movement of a snake through long grass.

Some of the most successful SAS undercover operators were the Fijian members of the regiment, who because of their dark caste could successfully blend into the local populace and move unhindered through the streets and marketplaces of Crater and Sheikh Othman. The SAS also had the shared use, along with other British military units, of the Cemetery Valley shooting range which was based at the foot of the Jebel Shamsam and was located on an ancient Arab burial site. Compared to today's modern CQB ranges it was a very rudimentary affair and consisted of a nearby armoury, a twenty-five metre firing range and a dozen metal target holders buried in the ground, with all targets being the standard figure targets. Interestingly there was no backstop, instead rounds merely carried on until they lost energy or occasionally 'zinged' off the craggy rocks surrounding the base of the Jebel.

The SAS had exclusive use of the range in the afternoons, a time when there were no other units allowed in for reasons of operational security. It is interesting to note that while other units used the range perhaps several times a week, the SAS counter-terrorist team were there everyday, training and refining their CQB tactics. Using a variety of weapons for counter-terrorist operations such as the pistol and sub-machine gun, the SAS soldiers would run through fast concealed weapon draws and firing, and similar to the Grant-Taylor benchmark, they were expected to hit consistently and accurately.

Subsequently the SAS proactive tactics to counter these terror attacks, consisted of the classic 'tether the goat, to catch the tiger' ruse. One SAS man, dressed openly in a British officer's uniform, would wander among the local populace in the high-risk areas of Crater and Sheik Othman, thus making himself an irresistible target for the terrorists. He was the goat. He would be followed in a classic protective surveillance operation by members of the SAS counter-terrorist team, again disguised in Arab garb, which would be ready to carry out fast draws and even faster shooting to take out the terrorist before he could attack the British VIP.

On 30 November 1967 the British finally pulled out, leaving Aden and the rest of the FSA under NLF control, but for the special forces units it had given them something invaluable—their first taste of undercover and counter-terrorist operations and training. Something that they would return to again and again over the next few decades, and something they would continually adapt, evolve and begin to write a new set of rules for.

The Counter-Revolutionary Warfare (CRW) wing was the SAS's answer to the growing terrorist threat of the 1960s and '70s when all manner of revolutionaries were butchering and bombing their way across Europe and the Middle East. CRW had started as a conduit of the bodyguard training team, but would eventually go on to grow and encompass a wide range of skills, including training and operations in the fields of VIP protection, counter-terrorism and special projects.

In the late 1960s the SAS was going through a period of innovative change, due in no small part to its newly appointed Commanding Officer Lieutenant-Colonel John Slim, and on the international stage SAS instructors would regularly provide specialist training to various government entities in the arts of close protection (bodyguard), security and hostage rescue. With the basic principles of counter-terrorist operations and hostage rescue being constantly refined and updated by the CRW team, the next phase was to have the very best in weapons, training equipment and logistical support in place.

An example of these technical improvements can be seen in the selection of the primary weapon for its CRW operations. Up until the early 1960s the SAS had been using a variety of ageing weapons such as the American Ingram M10 sub-machine gun, a compact weapon that fired a .45 calibre round. However the consensus within the CRW Wing was that the M10 was unsuitable for the operational tasks that the SAS would need it for, and as such they set about the search for a more modern weapon that offered power, versatility and reliability.

After a trawl of the world's arms manufacturers, the weapon that was chosen was the German made Heckler and Koch 9-mm MP5 sub-machine gun. Initial production of the MP5 had began in 1964 and it was subsequently first trialled by the West German border police and special forces units.

The weapon was light, robust, and came with a 30-round magazine. Its effective range was up to 200 metres and it also had the added advantage of a single, three-round burst or fully automatic rate of fire, making it versatile for any number of situations. Over the past forty years the H&K MP5, and its variants, has become the standard weapon of numerous nations' special forces and elite police units.

Perhaps the most famous part of the SAS counter-terrorist training was the CQB building which was located at the regiment's base in Hereford. Known inside the regiment as the 'killing house', it was based on the ideas of Fairbairn, Sykes and Grant-Taylor's mystery shoots.

The CQB building was a two storey, eight-roomed house that was equipped with specially made rubber lined walls to absorb bullets. The rooms were kitted out with furniture, pictures, ornaments and general facilities. Eventually with the advent of video technology, cameras would be placed in the various rooms for later debriefs and critiques of the assault team's performance. Whereas the main premise of an assault house was the same as in Fairbairn's day, the SAS specialist role was now more diverse and required a different approach to room combat.

Fairbairn's mystery houses during Commando, SOE and OSS training operations were aimed at the gunman entering a building with the remit to eliminate any enemy agents or officers that were present. In short they were sent in to kill and not to be too concerned about any innocent parties that were caught in the cross-fire.

However the modern SAS had to do much more than simply stalk an enemy and then shoot them dead. They had to plan and train for terrorist elimination certainly, but also hostage rescue of innocent civilians and snatch squads to arrest war criminals and terrorists. An example of a hostage rescue training scenario would have the SAS assault team approaching the building (either covertly or in a rapid attack) then use a suitable method of entry which may include shaped charges to blow the door out, or perhaps a specially loaded shotgun round to shatter the lock and hinges. Once entry was gained the assault team would throw in stun grenades and almost instantly enter, identifying targets and eliminating them. All this would be a dark, cramped and disorientating environment. Quite often the assault team would be firing accurately at targets mere inches from their fellow team members.

This type of specialist VIP protection and counter terrorist training was later offered to various friendly nations that were keen to set up their own counter-terrorist forces and Colonel Charlie Beckwith's American counter-terrorist unit, Delta Force, the German Grenzschutzgruppe 9 (GSG-9), and a host of lesser known Middle Eastern special forces were all trained along SAS lines. At home during the 1970s a number of British organisations also benefited from this type of training including Royal Protection and Royal Military Police personnel in the area of bodyguard and VIP protection instruction.

Counter-terrorism training was provided for the 14th Intelligence Company, the British military's elite undercover unit operating in Northern Ireland, as well as many regional police firearms units in specialist firearms training and hostage rescue operations. Not that the CRW Training Wing rested on their laurels regarding improving what they had so far achieved. Indeed, over many years, the SAS CQB method was continually altered, adapted and improved. For example, during the 1970s and '80s there was a move towards the practical shooting methods of sporting and competition shooting that utilised the weaver stance.

The Weaver Stance was considered at one time the cutting edge of practical shooting and provided the shooter with a stable platform with which to gain accurate shots on target within a given range and timeframe. And while the Weaver Stance and its variants were exceptional in a certain context, (for example in sporting and competition shooting), it clearly failed to take into account the effects of fear, adrenalin, limited reaction time and restrictive environments. So, as with most training methods, the SAS did what it does best—it took the best aspects of a given technique and adapted it to how they could use them more effectively for their own operational tasks. Sighted fire, it seems, was the 'old new thing'.

During the 1980s, and with numerous terrorist groups being active in Europe, there were two SAS counter-terrorism operations that stood out for their effective use of CQB and the wisdom of clinical targeted shooting methods. The first was the Iranian Embassy siege, which took place from 30 April to 5 May 1980, after a group of six armed men stormed the Iranian Embassy in South Kensington, London.

It is not the intention to go into the minute detail of the hostage rescue operation that took place in May 1980, as that has been covered numerous times before in many, many excellent publications. But it is relevant for us to look at some of the actual accounts of CQB that took place inside the building of 16 Princess Gate, South Kensington, London. The SAS rescue operation was known as Operation Nimrod and consisted of two assault teams, red and blue, that were to enter simultaneously from the front and rear windows, working their way through the building, clearing the rooms of terrorists and moving the hostages to safety. The assault started at 1923 hours on 5 May 1980. Eleven minutes later, Operation Nimrod was over.

The casualty list included one hostage that was killed during the assault, two hostages, one SAS man wounded, and five terrorists killed with one being captured. However, even for the SAS, not all operations go smoothly. 'No plan survives contact with the enemy' as Clausewitz famously stated, but even when things went awry, the professionalism and expert training of the SAS assault team came into play.

When the initial front assault began, the SAS team threw in a series of 'flash-bang' stun grenades to subdue anyone hiding inside the various rooms. Unfortunately because of the high concentration of magnesium powder and mercury inside them they ignited the heavy curtains, which soon become engulfed in flames. One SAS trooper, who later won the Queen's Gallantry Medal for his part in Nimrod, caught fire and was forced to rip off his respirator and hood before carrying on with his part in the assault. Once he had entered the building he became aware of a terrorist on the opposite side of the room.

The SAS man immediately brought his MP5 up to fire, depressed the trigger and received a dead man's click. This is that heart-stopping moment when the weapon has jammed and the operator has to decide whether to clear the malfunction or transition to another weapon. In this case the SAS trooper chose, wisely, the latter and transitioned to his sidearm, the trusty 9 mm Browning. By this time the terrorist had enough of a head start to flee from the room and was headed to the location of some of the hostages on that floor. In his hand was a Russian made fragmentation grenade. It seems evident that that the terrorist was intent on murdering the innocents. He never made it. The SAS man, in close pursuit, went for a head-shot and the terrorist fell lifelessly to the floor. He then moved the hostages through the building to the exit and safety.

Another example of responding effectively to an ever changing hostage rescue situation can be seen by a fellow assault team member who was stationed on the embassy's main staircase. His role was to be part of a team responsible for moving a stream of rescued hostages along and out into the exit. As they were moved along, one SAS man is said to have identified a terrorist that had hidden among the hostages and alerted the rest of his squad. The terrorist was immediately bundled down the staircase at speed, before one trooper spotted another fragmentation grenade concealed in the man's hand.

However because of the terrorists' positioning, there were hostages and other SAS soldiers in the way and the trooper could not fire. Instead he made the inspired decision to club the man with the butt of his sub machine gun, causing him to drop and roll to the bottom of the stairs. This was closely followed by two SAS troopers firing into his body to ensure that he could not detonate the grenade.

The man was later identified as Faisal, the second-in-command of the terrorists. These two examples, of which there were undoubtedly many more, showcase the need for concise training, maturity on behalf of the operator and the confidence to change tactics and adapt when the situation calls for it. It also gave clear validity to the SAS CQB methods.

Operation Nimrod was a resounding success for the special projects team and catapulted the SAS to the forefront of the British public's mind, transforming the special forces into, at times, almost mythical supermen. It also sent a very clear message out to the international terrorist community that said, Great Britain is protected.

The second example of effective CQB on a counter terrorist operation took place eight years later in March 1988. This operation occurred on the international stage, in a location that one would not immediately associate with Irish terrorism. Codenamed Operation FLAVIUS, its task was to halt a Provisional Irish Republican Army (PIRA) bomb attack that was to be carried out in the heart of Gibraltar. The targets were to be the band members of the Royal Anglian Regiment. They would assemble for the parade in the centre of town as part of the changing of the guard outside the governor's mansion. The method of attack was to be a car bomb that was to be detonated remotely by an IRA Active Service Unit (ASU).

The ASU consisted of three experienced IRA terrorists, Danny McCann, Sean Savage and Mairead Farrell who had been tracked and placed under surveillance by British Security Service and the Spanish police, while the trio had been on various reconnaissance trips in the run up to the planned bomb attack.

The original plan for the counter-terrorist operation was meant to be a hard arrest that was to be carried out by a plain-clothes SAS Special Projects Team. The team would isolate the ASU, detain them and then hand them over to the Spanish Police. However due to the terrorists' erratic behaviour it ended with the SAS teams opening fire on the IRA ASU members. This would later give rise to claims of a Government sponsored shoot-to-kill policy.

Prior to the start of the operation, the SAS had been issued with the rules of engagement and this included the initial objective of arresting the ASU, but if members of the public or security services' lives were put in danger (or believed to be about to be put in danger) then the SAS could open fire, without warning, to negate the threat.

The plain-clothes SAS teams were issued with the standard 9 mm Browning, covert communications and set off around the town to follow the IRA unit. Before long, McCann and Farrell had split off from Savage, with the two groups heading off to different parts of town. Closely following behind were two SAS teams, each consisting of two soldiers. The first engagement took place at 1542 and involved McCann and Farrell. McCann had been spooked by a passing police car with its sirens going. He turned around and made eye contact with one of the two SAS men that were following behind, no more than three yards away.

The SAS soldier claimed that McCann made an aggressive body motion, perhaps going for a weapon or detonator button, when he shot him with a single round in the back. He then turned his attention to Farrell, who had made a grab for her handbag, whom he also fired a single round at, again into her back. As both McCann and Farrell started to go down, this was followed by a further three shots into McCann—one to the body, two to the head—as well as seven more shots fired at both terrorists by both soldiers. Both SAS men later claimed that they feared that Farrell may still have been able to depress a detonator button and initiate the suspected device.

As the shots rang out a mere 100 yards away Sean Savage, by now heading in a different direction, turned and reacted to the volley of gunfire. As he turned, his hand made a motion as if he was reaching for his trouser pocket, and with the information that he could have been armed with a remote detonator, the SAS soldiers drew their weapons. However a female pedestrian was between Savage and the SAS team. Using techniques that had been perfected for bodyguard training, the SAS soldier moved her out of the way with one hand whilst drawing and firing with the other. Both SAS men put a total of fifteen rounds into Savage.

The engagement is, following the legal case, now a matter of detailed public record and has been written about by many authors over the past twenty years, but what it shows is the rapidity in which a close quarter contact can happen. It also shows that such an intense and urgent action cannot be effectively portrayed in a clinical written description. What does happen is that the training of the operator kicks in and, as he has been taught, he acts quickly, effectively and ruthlessly. It can be over in a matter of seconds.

In the situation of Operation Flavius, once the SAS feared that the ASU posed a reasonable threat to the security forces and/or innocent parties, any delay or hesitation could have been catastrophic. This is even more relevant when there is credible intelligence that a remote detonation device could be active in the area, and as such the need to act and negate the threat is paramount.

As the investigation progressed the evidence suggested that the IRA team were not armed with remote detonators and were in fact on a reconnaissance run for a future attack. The actual car bomb was found the next day in Marbella, loaded with over sixty pounds of Semtex.

These two examples are mere snapshots of the type of CQB work that goes on within special forces and counter-terrorism operations. For the most part these operations are justifiably kept secret, and the general public never get to hear of them. They never hear about the bomb that does not explode, the insurgent that mysteriously disappears, the terrorist ambush that never happens.

As we have seen, what was needed for the difficult area of hostage rescue and counter-terrorist operations was pin-point accuracy and the clinical selection of hostile targets in a restrictive environment. This was akin to a surgeon carefully removing a difficult-to-access cancer. In a crowded room combat environment, or in a busy civilian thoroughfare it could mean the difference between cleanly taking out a terrorist and leaving a civilian alive and unharmed. Dead terrorists and live hostages was the hope.

However, we should also remember that they do things slightly different in the SAS compared to the rest of the British Army. The individual SAS operator, having absorbed the fundamental principles of CQB, will be a seasoned, and mature soldier, who is able to adapt the system to his ability of instant reaction, posture and determination.

In the twenty-first century the current state of modern CQB training is multi-faceted and multi-technique driven. This has been assisted over the past thirty years in no small part due to the advancement of technology; both in regards to the training equipment available, and in the technical improvements in the areas of tactical equipment and in modern ballistics. From the training equipment aspect, probably one of the best training aids has been the creation of airsoft and simunition and its proliferation throughout the professional and civilian training environments.

Whereas previously, tactical firearms training would consist of nothing more than range work, perhaps at multi-directional targets, with the advent of simunition, the tactical firearms specialist is now able to safely integrate unarmed combat draws, grappling draws, and firing at a live (perhaps even charging) attacker to make the training environment much more realistic and interactive.

Wartime CQB was adapted and improved upon postwar for a new generation of CQB operators by those pioneers of the special forces. In the postwar era it was a response to dealing with the new threat of undercover warfare and counter-terrorism. But as has been previously stated, threats are constantly evolving and changing, enemies learn and adapt too, and the professional CQB specialist also has to adapt, learn new skills and improve. To remain locked into a fixed position is to court death.

By contrast, the modern CQB operator has to be a more rounded fighter than simply being a gunman. Rather than being seen as a niche specialist of one discipline, the modern operator trains in a variety of skills, each complementing and aiding the other. He will have knowledge of unarmed combat, grappling, transitioning, as well as edged weapon and firearms work. Each of these skills he integrates seamlessly into his close quarter combat training.

Aside from the obvious technological advances over recent years such as laser-aiming, shooting simulators, the creation of lightweight Kydex holsters and tactical rigs, the advent of force-on-force training using airsoft weapons and simunition cartridges stands out head and shoulders above the rest.

Force on Force (FOF) is geared towards a more interactive experience for the modern combative operator and as well as combining firearms training, also give the participants the opportunity to deal with simulated attacks from unarmed, edged weapon and impact weapons.

The scenarios can be anything from the 'good guy gunman' having to assess a tactical situation such as a rushing knife attacker, and then access and deploy his firearm to quickly deal with the assault, to a team tactic drill whereby the team storms a building to eliminate terrorists. The beauty of this FOF training is that the 'bad guys' are more than static paper targets, they are a living breathing enemy that have to act out the reality of a given situation.

This type of training has largely shifted the focus away from just shooting paper targets on the range, to a more physical and diverse aspect of close quarter firearms work. It has also ensured that the lazy operators either have to re-think their combative strategy and take a more robust attitude to CQB, rather than simply relying on a firearm to deal with every tactical problem. The days of the operator extolling the 'I don't need to be fit or to be able to fight or to use a knife, because I've got a gun' attitude are long over. Not that range work is obsolete, far, far from it, but at least there is a balance in place between training marksmanship and training close combat.

Over the past thirty years, the wheel has turned numerous times regarding which is the best system to use for CQB pistol work—point shooting or sighted fire. Firearms trainers have an almost religious like zeal about endorsing their chosen system. During the 1970s and 1980s, sighted fire training was in vogue, primarily due to the influence of numerous American firearms trainers that endorsed that system mainly for sporting competitions. However, from the 1990s onwards, there has been resurgence in the art of point shooting, in no small part due to its effectiveness at close quarters for both military and civilian self-protection applications, as well as the latter day interest in Fairbairn and Sykes and the wartime methods.

So for the trainee, which system should be taught as part of their close combat firearms work? For me it has always been a pointless argument. The simple answer is both.

Point shooting and sighted fire are not mutually exclusive for close combat, they both have merit, and used in the correct arena and context they can be a devastating combination. They are, in effect, two sides of the same coin, and for the firearms exponent to say he will only use one over the other, is akin to a martial artist saying that he will only ever kick in combat and never use punches, throws, or grapples. In short it is cutting your nose off to spite your face.

The modern day CQB operator, whether civilian, military, police, or government, now has a more diverse range of skills. He is so much more than a blunt instrument to be used physically. He is geared not just towards weapons and combative skills, but also will have knowledge of tactical driving, trauma management, surveillance and counter-surveillance, languages, intelligence gathering, and covert communications.

In many respects the majority of the hard work for modern CQB has already been done. The experience, concepts, and tactics, have already been borne out on the streets of Shanghai, Aden, Palestine, Northern Ireland, and Europe, and are still as valid today as they were more than eighty years ago.

What is required today of the modern operator, is his need to be technically proficient, faster, fitter, and more tactically aware. After all he is much more than just a machine; he has to be able to know when to pull the trigger, or not, depending on how the situation in hand develops. And so what had started as a shooting method on the battlefields of the First World War, had been taken up and used by the colonial police of Shanghai, adopted by the commandos and secret services during the Second World War, and which was eventually re-evaluated and updated by the postwar SAS, now provides the CQB operator with the fundamental skills and empirical knowledge to be able to use this effectively in a modern combative environment.

I also have no doubt that the search, adaptation, and refinement of these particular set of skills will continue to grow and develop for generations to come, and that this widespread holistic and practical approach to modern CQB, and its tactical usage, is something that Colonel Hector Grant-Taylor would have approved of wholeheartedly.

CHAPTER NINE:

Conclusion: Anatomy
of an Investigation

In a wilderness of mirrors, who can you trust?
James Jesus Angleton, CIA Counter-Intelligence Chief

This book began life as a treatise on the finer points of CQB shooting, and I hope that it still is in many ways. But because of the protagonist at its heart, it eventually grew into a whodunit mystery, or more accurately a who-was-he mystery. There were many blind alleys, false leads, and downright mistruths spread by Grant-Taylor over the course of his life, and trying to untangle fact from fiction took up the greater part of the research for this book.

When I first started researching Grant-Taylor's life, I was expecting it to be a pretty straight-forward information gathering affair. After all we had all the information, didn't we? Upper class gentleman from Scotland, check. Taught the FBI, check. Worked with the commandos and shot down a group of Luftwaffe, check. Disappeared after the war, check. It seemed like a clear case. Then things started not to add up. A piece of information here that did not tally with a piece of information there. It soon became apparent that the man known as Leonard Hector Grant-Taylor did not actually exist. In a sense that made it even more of an interesting project than I had previously thought.

So my first problem was, how do you discover the true identity of a man living under a false name, especially when all the individuals involved were long since dead? After all, in theory he could have been a John Smith or a hundred other variations on a random name. I have been active in the private investigation industry for well over a decade, and in that time I have worked on corporate fraud, traced missing persons, done background checks, undercover infiltration work, covert surveillance operations and everything in between.

From this, experience has shown me that every job is unique. Of course they all run a certain way and normally have a structured outcome, but along the investigation path there are many side roads that can lead you down a dead end and waste many man hours, resources and finance. The trick for the investigator is to recognise as early as possible the red herrings from the seam of gold. I would like to be able to tell you that there was a proven method, a clear route through to discovering the truth—after all, in the detective TV shows it happens over an hour and a half—but unfortunately I can't. It was a long, long slog and was an organic process with no information coming in a linear way. Some of it was luck, and some of it came from just having a sense of how Grant-Taylor was thinking at various points in his life.

The author Lee Child, who is best known for his Jack Reacher character, states that the best skill an investigator can have is empathy with the person they are tracking. I could not agree more. You have to be able to put yourself in his shoes and reason out why he would do certain things. To track a man, especially a long dead one, is almost a form of alchemy. As well as the empathy angle, an experienced investigator has a wide range of assets at his disposal in order to gain accurate information. We should also include the obvious use of confidential informants and accurate open sources, coupled with one of the biggest assets over the past twenty years—the use of online technology. It has opened up a previously unavailable level of information that, while not necessarily giving the investigator the whole picture, can quite often give them a nudge in the right direction or at the very least rule out what is not relevant.

Not that people who want to hide, then as now, make it easy for the investigator. If someone wants to disappear then it is relatively easy to do so. However that kind of disappearing act usually requires a vast amount of money to vanish and a certain type of mind-set to see it through. Not everyone is tough enough or committed enough, and even if they are it is only a matter of time, and perseverance, on behalf of a professional investigator before he can narrow down the leads and searches and tracks his man to lair.

The reader will probably note that quite early on in the book, I no longer continued to refer to Grant-Taylor by his original name of Leonard Taylor. My reasons were not purely for practicality and continuity, but also for the very reason that, like Grant-Taylor himself, I wanted to convey how relatively quickly and ruthlessly he shed his skin and discarded his original identity. He cast off Leonard Taylor, and does not seem to have looked back. We now know, of course, that for many a year he was living a lie, not just regarding his background, but also in the direction that his life was heading. False identities, financial impropriety, bigamy, prison. In many ways he considered himself a lost cause, perhaps even a failure, with what he had hoped to achieve for himself in his youth being replaced by the life of mistakes that he had been handed. Fate is inexorable it would seem.

Therefore, while Grant-Taylor undoubtedly did much to disguise his identity over the course of his life, perhaps hoping to change his destiny completely, fundamentally it seems obvious that he was a man on a journey. Unfortunately that journey took him through his youth and manhood, and did not reach its conclusion until he finally reached late middle age. Here then, in the late 1940s, he was finally contented and at a place where he was happiest, both geographically and as a man.

Of course, in researching any book there are always the supporting characters that have to be investigated so as to provide a bigger and more comprehensive picture of the main protagonist's life and events. In *At Close Quarters* we have a cast that are just as impressive and fascinating as Grant-Taylor himself, and each of them had a mini-investigation to their names. For most of the individuals mentioned in this book it was relatively easy to discover their backgrounds, and where they fitted in to the big picture as many had a semi-public persona—General William Slim, William Fairbairn, Eric Anthony Sykes, Hermione Ranfurly, John Slim, etc.

However, in the case of Kathleen Grant-Taylor, there was very little information available, and out of all the people that I had to investigate her story was probably the most difficult to track down. In many ways she was just as much of an enigma as her 'husband.' Of Grant-Taylor's story, I believe that in the years to come, and with the release of even more public records, there will be more snippets relating to his life for future researchers to dig deeper into if they so choose. I hope they do, and I hope that *At Close Quarters* acts as the nexus from which to build all future information upon.

With *At Close Quarters* I wanted the opportunity to set the record straight regarding Grant-Taylor's relationship to Fairbairn, Sykes and SOE. I wanted it be accurate and informative certainly, without being too heavy in overly complex detail. More importantly, I also wanted to make it accessible to the general public. My overall aim was for the book to appeal to people with no knowledge of this milieu. I wanted to reach an audience of historians, Second World War military aficionados, and students of CQB, not just a small clique of niche enthusiasts. Once the true story of Grant-Taylor started to come to light I soon realised that his life was worthy of the whole book in itself, not just about his firearms work, and from that point on *At Close Quarters* was Grant-Taylor's book.

There are many things that are required of an instructor, especially an instructor whose knowledge may one day save the lives of his students, and for the man known as Grant-Taylor, his main asset was his skill in being able to sell the confidence behind the technique. Grant-Taylor is what I would term an 'instructor's, instructor.' Many instructors know their subject matter in depth, but not every one of them has the sheer gravitas and charisma to get the information across in such a clear and bold method. His lectures provided the adrenaline and fighting spirit to enable a young man who had never used a firearm in lethal combat, the wherewithal to be able to use it competently, and in a deadly manner.

Aside from his teaching ability, there can be no doubt about Grant-Taylor's skills with a pistol. Was he a natural? Possibly, he was certainly consistent with his shooting on the range if we are to believe the anecdotal evidence from people who trained under him. But more importantly even if he was not, his shooting ability does nothing but endorse how effective the point shooting method that he utilised actually was. People with no natural talent could learn this method and be effective in a very short space of time. And while Fairbairn went on to train perhaps hundreds of SOE and OSS personnel in this close quarter shooting method, Grant-Taylor, by comparison, went on to train and pass his expertise on to perhaps three times that number through his work with the commandos, special forces, regular military and various police forces.

But what of the modern applications of the Grant-Taylor system? Does it still have merit and are its principles still relevant today? I believe so, and for the past decade or more I have integrated many of his teachings—both in terms of mindset and tactics—into my own training, whilst also trying

134

to pass this information on to others who may not be so familiar with his methods. This research project into his true life story also spawned the research and analysis of his shooting methods, and after many years of learning from people who had been taught directly by the man himself, and from tracking down previously unseen material, it seemed prudent to provide an opportunity for others to study them also.

The initial Grant-Taylor lecture took place in August 2005 when our close combat training team presented the principles, techniques and tactics that Grant-Taylor had espoused to a small workshop of point shooting practitioners. However in the summer of 2012 (through to the summer of 2013), I was fortunate enough to be invited to run a further series of Grant-Taylor Lectures that showcased his CQB shooting style and how it had evolved from the wartime syllabus, through to the special forces methods of the 1960s and on to the modern CQB firearms training that is widely in use today. We presented a number of these training lectures to suitably qualified attendees and worked through the CQB techniques with handguns, sub-machine guns, pump-action shotguns and a variety of airsoft and simunition training weapons. The tools may change, but the basic principles remain the same.

The first 2012 Grant-Taylor CQB Lecture took place at a UK Anti-Terrorist Firearms training facility. In attendance on this initial course were a specially invited group of former military, police close protection personnel and specialist firearms officers. All had many years service and equally had a wide range of experience and skills. For some of the team it was a refresher, as it is something they had been doing for years, and for others it was a new learning journey.

Throughout these training programmes we had the opportunity to look at all the theories and practical applications of the Grant-Taylor wartime syllabus, starting with a dry-fire session, then moving onto live fire shooting, before slowly adding in tactical movement, various distances, and of course, quick draw applications.

As this point shooting lecture was meant to be about a progressive system, we would discuss how certain UK military units had taken the original applications formulated by Grant-Taylor and evolved them for their own unique remits and theatres of operations, namely using a two handed stance to point shoot.

On a personal note, this is a stance and method I have always felt comfortable with for many years, even when I have studied new methods, instinctively I have still reverted back to this two handed, aggressive, shooting stance. From there it was back to the firing line to go over everything that had been discussed and to put it into practical application on the range. Over a relatively short period of time the point shooting method quickly became second nature, and was borne out by consistent shots to the centre of mass on the targets.

For the next module we would then move indoors, more specifically to a state of the art CQB killing house—in modern politically correct parlance the 'dynamic intervention building'—or what Grant-Taylor would have termed his execution shed. Here the team would enter the building one by one, find the appropriate room and engage the targets that presented themselves as a threat. First in a covert method of entry, and finally in a 'crash and bash' room storming with all guns a blazing. We would throw everything at them—noise, sound effects, flashing lights, dark rooms and general encumbrance during the method of entry phase.

On some of these modules there were several interesting outcomes. On one occasion, the students entered and stood stock still in the doorway, thus providing a tantalising silhouette target framed perfectly with the light behind them and then try to pick off the targets from this static shooting position. This was both unsatisfactory, and would have been lethal for them in a real combat environment.

The training team reiterated Grant-Taylor's basic rules for room combat, namely the 'point of domination' as well as dominating the room with aggressive forward movement. Then we demonstrated how those principles should be applied by charging into the room, and virtually hunting down the targets, not giving them time to react. When we ran the students through it again, with these principles now fresh in their minds, we had a more aggressive outcome, and the targets were decimated in a matter of seconds. After each drill we would do an overall debrief of how we could be quicker, faster, and more accurate when storming the room. We would also add in numerous VIP protection drills that included the use of dealing with hostile crowds, close range attacks, and accurate target acquisition. This was then integrated into a street scenario drill. First we double checked that the weapons were not loaded so as to conduct dry-fire training. Next we partnered the group up into pairs and on the signal a given shooter had to move aside various innocent members of the crowd—via a push, takedown or verbal command—in order to have a clear shot at his partner (the terrorist).

136

On a practical note we should remember that both the Grant-Taylor method or indeed even Fairbairn's 'shooting to live' training were a sign of the times that they were created in. No system can survive intact in a vacuum indefinitely. A system once created will have to grow, expand, retract, evolve or it will ultimately die, and while many of the wartime point shooting and close combat principles are still valid and are still applied, there have been definite advances in technology, ergonomics and tactics over the last sixty years of close combat pistol training.

Our overall aim on these lectures was to give an accurate portrayal of Grant-Taylor and who he actually was, rather than the misinformation that has found its way into some material over recent years, and obviously to promote the point shooting system, as a viable means of CQB that Grant-Taylor had taught.

The latter we certainly did, at least among the various groups of experienced personnel who we had to work with over the period of a year. The feedback we received was positive, and several mentioned that they would be incorporating elements of the training methods they had been taught into their own syllabuses. As for the former, the man himself, I hope you have at least an inkling of who he was and what lay behind him from reading the preceding chapters.

Grant-Taylor was a complex and flawed human being—of that there is no doubt. In many respects he was a weak and vain man that did many questionable things, and if you are hoping that you will get to know the man intimately—and know what made him tick—from reading this book, I fear that you will be disappointed. I do not think anyone knew the real man, not his wives, friends, nor fellow soldiers. Hector Grant-Taylor was a creation cooked up by a desperate man at a desperate time in his life, a born improviser who could turn a story on its head and talk his way out of trouble to better his own ends. He was a man that was constantly updating himself.

In modern terms there are many of Grant-Taylor's characteristics that would brand him a sociopath, or at the very least for him to have sociopathic tendencies. He was a master of influence and deception, charming, highly intelligent, dominant, and while in his youth he may have been concerned about his lack of conscience in some of his more extreme decisions, by late adulthood he had learned to suppress such matters and carry on regardless. He was a man of many masks, and one that was certainly driven, by greed, fear or ambition, we will never now.

Perhaps even he did not know. That is what has made the character of Grant-Taylor to be so fascinating and elusive.

Grant-Taylor was a man of his time in that he believed in colonial rule, and the power of the British Empire as so many of his generation had been brought up to do so. More importantly, he was a man born *out* of his time. He was a traveller, an adventurer, a lover of women, a manipulator of men. If he had been born fifty years earlier, and on a different continent, he would have been a big game hunter in Africa, a China trader in Asia, or riding a stagecoach across the plains of Texas. History always throws up such men. In peacetime they are unruly, troublemakers, surly, and more often than not heading for a lifetime in the gutter or in jail.

However in wartime, some men come into their own and excel. They crave action, excitement, and the comradeship of their brothers-in-arms. Grant-Taylor was such a man, but it is my firm belief that throughout their lives even flawed human beings have at least one shot at redemption. Everyone deserves at least one opportunity to make amends for past failures. For Grant-Taylor that chance of redemption came during the war of 1939-1945.

Despite all the hyperbole, all the falsehoods, all the lies, Grant-Taylor believed in what he was doing. He was helping those boys, some of them no more than teenagers at the time, with a chance to survive. To fight, survive and live. While some may justifiably criticise his morals, I believe that at the forefront of any supposed deceptions, of which there were many, was that ultimate moral compass that said to the soldiers of the armed forces of Britain, America and Asia, 'I will give you the best chance that I can.'

Greater love hath no man than this, that a man lay down his life for his friends.

John 15:13

Advice for Researchers and the *Very* Curious Tale of Mr William Pilkington

Inquisitorem Caveat (Researcher Beware)

And so Grant-Taylor's story has been told. I hope you enjoyed it. In a sense this epilogue really has nothing to do with the main body of the book, as it really only touches obliquely on the subject of Grant-Taylor. So please do not confuse the two.

This epilogue is about the subject of researching a book and its many pitfalls, especially when dealing with limited information, very shaky anecdotal testimony and a mass of people telling you 'no you're wrong about that, when you know 100 per cent that you are right about it. It is a minefield. And that is before we even get to the thorny subject of actually getting the book published.

Most research projects start off on one path and eventually end up on a completely different one by the end of the journey. The book that I started many, many, years ago is not the one that you hold in your hands. It went through numerous changes to get to where it is now. So how did it begin? It began, like most investigations, with a mystery.

The world of Second World War close combat history and research is littered, it would seem, with an awful lot of falsehood, sheer fantasy and the occasional Walter Mitty. Some people buy into it with a fervour, while others are desperately trying to see through the smoke and mirrors to get to the truth.

At Close Quarters was originally going to be about W. E. Fairbairn's wartime group of twelve instructors, a cadre that he allegedly put together to go out and teach various elements of the Army and Home Guard in the invasion summer of 1940. Grant-Taylor is often promoted as being one of those, hence my initial interest in the twelve. This was partly the reason that I began the research—due to this alleged connection. As we now know this was impossible as Grant-Taylor did not begin his military service until late 1940 and was not even in Scotland at the Paramilitary camps until 1941, and much of my subsequent research casts serious doubt on the supposed stories of the twelve-instructor cadre in July 1940.

So where to start finding out who these mysterious twelve actually were? There had been little in the way of hard evidence since the end of the war, and only rumours based on wishful thinking over the past decade. The majority of the evidence relating to Fairbairn's twelve is often based on the assumption that those Second World War close combat instructors who have a profile today, and who were around during that time, were all involved. This consisted of nothing more than hearsay and one vital piece of written documentation, *The Anti-Invasion Measures of Defence Tactics: Notes for Instructors* (AIMDT/NI).

The AIMDT/NI is alleged to have been written as a morale-boosting pamphlet by Fairbairn in July 1940. It was said to have been handed out to his twelve instructors in order that they could pass the rhetoric on in their own lectures to various units of the Home Guard, Army, Navy, etc. In it, Fairbairn supposedly endorses the close combat work of a Mr (William) Pilkington and a Mr Carr, allegedly two instructors on the summer 1940 close combat course. Mr Carr has never truly been identified, but the other name, that of Mr Pilkington has become widely known in Second World War combative research circles over the past twenty years.

In the document Fairbairn states that 'I suggest that all instructors take extra training from Mr (William) Pilkington in his highly lethal staff, stick and baton system. This should be passed on to the public, as should his other contribution of improvised self defence system. British Forces have already been given training in these systems.' High praise indeed from Captain Fairbairn.

It is rather strange that this document never reappears anywhere else, not in the Imperial War Museum, not in the National Archives, not in W. E. Fairbairn's SOE file. Nowhere. It is also strange that of all the twelve instructors only William Pilkington is given his full name and the other gentleman is only referred to as Mr Carr. Not even a rank is given for either, only the lone title of 'Mr'. So who was this lethal unarmed combat and weapons expert that operated for SOE? William 'Bill' Pilkington promoted himself as the son of a police inspector who had been on stage at the Argyle Theatre, Birkenhead, on the night that Hitler had declared war. He attended Liverpool University, but later dropped out to pursue an acting career. After enlisting, he is said to have worked closely with Major Colin Gubbins during the operations in Norway, in which Pilkington and another soldier are said to have killed two quislings—with a pistol and a knife—when their cover was blown during a reconnaissance operation. He later stated that they were part of a top-secret unit called No. 1 independent-field intelligence unit and that he had been Gubbins' right-hand-man and interpreter during operations in Norway.

He later took part in the Dunkirk evacuations before being recruited, by Gubbins, to work as a trainee silent killing instructor under Fairbairn and Sykes for SOE, in which he was allowed to teach, personally by Fairbairn, Pilkington's own stick, staff and baton methods of close quarter combat. He claimed he took part in the initial training cadre in the summer of 1940 before being sent out across Britain to teach the Home Guard and the secret Auxiliary Units (AU) of the Home Guard. Later he would claim that he taught the young Princess Elizabeth unarmed combat during her time with the ATS and showed Prime Minister Winston Churchill how to fire a Sten gun.

In late 1941 he claimed that he was recruited to be trained at Pentonville Prison, by Albert Pierrepoint, to be an executioner and hangman in case of an attempted invasion of Great Britain, the theory being that they would have to hang British traitors who had sided with the Nazis. He also stated that he was at one time called upon by MI5 to interrogate a Norwegian sailor who had been found wandering around Glasgow docks and who the authorities suspected was a German spy. Pilkington, who did indeed speak Norwegian, due to his mother being from Norway, allegedly questioned the man before turning him over to MI5 to be arrested and hanged.

In 1942 Pilkington was supposedly sent to the Middle East, received a commission as a Lieutenant, sent to language school to learn Arabic and was used by the 8th Army as a counter-intelligence officer to catch Nazi spies in North Africa and Egypt. Despite this, he still considered himself to be on the active list for SOE. As he put it himself, 'you never leave

SOE; once you're in they've got you for keeps.'

Whilst in the Middle East, he also claimed to be working with Major Roy Farran, rounding up and assassinating enemy agents, insurgents and militia groups. Of Farran, Pilkington stated of him that he was, 'a brilliant soldier and a great friend.' He also stated that the man was a 'freak', a 'nutter', and was just plain 'weird' on occasions.

In 1943, Pilkington stated that he had been dropped behind enemy lines in Italy for SOE to rally communist partisans to fight the fascists and had been promoted to Major and had also been a forward observation officer on Gold Beach on D-day during June 1944. Following this he had worked undercover, smoking out and interrogating German army intelligence infiltrators in Normandy and Cannes, and acquiring intelligence about enemy intentions. By the end of 1945 he was working in Berlin, once again in a counter-intelligence capacity, catching former Nazis, before working in the prosecutor's offices at the Nuremberg Trials, where he later, it was claimed, had been the assistant hangman at the execution of Josef Kramer, the notorious last commandant of the Nazi concentration camp at Bergen-Belsen.

Following his wartime service, Pilkington volunteered for the Palestine Police Force in the years leading up to the mandate in 1948. Again because of his 'special skills' he claimed to be recruited for intelligence work in which he stated he had been targeted by an Armenian assassin, shot at, and nearly blown up by terrorists when they bombed the King David Hotel. By the end of the mandate, he returned to civilian life to try his hand as a working actor in the theatre, TV and movies. Later on in his life he would go on to devote himself to various charities and good works and would receive a British Empire Medal. It is a fantastic, if somewhat busy, wartime story.

However, the truth about William Pilkington, his war service and his expertise in the Fairbairn close quarter combat method is somewhat different. William Pilkington was in fact born in Wallasey, Wirral on 9 December 1916. His father was Arthur Pilkington, who was serving as a private in the Army Service Corps when William was born. His mother was Johanne Pilkington, née Audland. Johanne and her family originally came from Norway but had settled in the north west of England some years before.

Arthur Pilkington was not a police inspector with any of the local forces, he was in fact a cashier's clerk in a local factory, and William, despite his later claims, had never attended Liverpool University. Prior to enlistment in the military in 1940, he had been working as a labourer in a seed mill and as a railway ticket inspector. There is no record of him ever having appeared at the Argyle Theatre. He enlisted for service on 15 February 1940 and was subsequently posted to No. 10 Training Battalion of the Railway Training Centre (Royal Engineers) to be trained as a 'pioneer brakesman and shunter'—He was to be a train driver. His responsibility was for the moving of logistical goods, personnel and munitions, and that is pretty much what he did for the remainder of the war. Between 1940 and 1944 he was a Royal Engineer Lance-Corporal that was stationed within the British Isles, being posted to various train yards and stations to help with the logistical supply of equipment for the war effort. In 1944 he was posted to the Middle East, again working as part of the Royal Engineers' train company, before returning to England for a year. It was during this time that he married and he was later promoted to sapper.

His military conduct was classed as exemplary, and his report states that 'Pilkington is a thoroughly competent and experienced railway traffic man, has plenty of drive and initiative and can always be relied upon in an emergency. Thoroughly honest and trustworthy.'

Having chosen to remain in the military after the end of hostilities, by 1946 Pilkington was sent to Palestine as part of 193 Railway Operating Company Royal Engineers. The 193's role was operating the railway system that did the day-to-day running, this also included maintenance of tracks and signalling duties. He remained on the Territorial Army reserve list as a train operator working in the Middle East, and Africa, until 1953 when his services were no longer required and he was returned back to the civilian world.

There were no undercover operations, no Fairbairn or Sykes, no silent killing, no dropped behind enemy lines. Pilkington had served his country well, something that he should have been proud of, but he served it as a train driver and railway inspector as part of the Royal Engineers.

From 1953 onwards Pilkington worked as a jobbing actor playing bit-parts in numerous TV dramas such as 'Z Cars' and 'Coronation Street'. To supplement his acting work he set himself up as a freelance private investigator. His calling card read 'William Pilkington—Investigator' and he was the company director of Pilkington's Detective Bureau and Security Service. Initially it was a large scale security service operation, employing at one time some 133 personnel, which had several large contracts providing security guards (or as one former employee called them 'cocky watchmen'), based primarily down at the docks and ports around Merseyside.

However sometime in the mid-1960s the business began to struggle and resulted in them losing a large contract to supply security staff. This is nothing unusual in the security industry. It can be a cutthroat business with rivals always keen to undercut and take away contracts from the original contractors. With the size of the business seriously depleted and struggling to make ends meet financially, Pilkington decided to concentrate solely on the investigation side of the business. Run from his home address in Mossley Hill, Liverpool, it was a small operation in which he offered such services as tracing and observations.

The private detective business was then—as it is now to some degree—virtually unregulated, with no checks as to the background of either the investigators or the clients. Jobs are taken on at a moment's notice with the investigator very rarely getting the whole picture as to why a client wants someone traced or followed and tracked to ground via means of foot surveillance. It was during this period that Bill Pilkington fell foul of the law. In January 1970 he was arrested and charged with entering a property in Formby belonging to a Mr Mariam Melewski, and stealing jewellery to the value of £86, which was a not inconsiderable sum in the early 1970s.

Mr Melewski had initially employed Bill Pilkington to make some general background enquiries about one of his employees. The initial consultation had taken place at the client's home address.

The prosecution stated that this was but one of a series of burglaries across the Merseyside region that had taken place between September 1969 and February 1970, in which the sum total of £3,000 had been stolen from well-to-do properties. They further explained that Bill Pilkington had visited these addresses in either a professional or social capacity, and had a special, but temporary relationship with the victim, in this case as either a client or acquaintance, and when he had the opportunity had stolen several items of value. Where there was no opportunity, he would act as the inside man and tip off several accomplices as to the state of security on the property, where any valuables were kept and so forth. The thieves would then return when the property was empty. From this, Bill Pilkington would receive a cut of the proceeds.

Despite pleading not guilty, and having raised the issue of being commended twice by the Chief Constable of the Liverpool Police Force for public action, he was found guilty on all charges. He was sentenced at Liverpool Crown Court in December 1970, and so at the age of fifty-five, Bill Pilkington began an eighteen-month prison sentence.

Throughout the 1970s and '80s he seems to have re-invented himself as a martial arts expert and talk of SOE, Fairbairn and Sykes, and the world of close quarter combat started to become a part of his patois. It is during this period that many of the falsehoods that he spread regarding this period of history, the personalities and the training that took place, began to grow and grow. They grew so much that they became accepted as fact.

William Pilkington, BEM, remained in the north-west for much of the remainder of his life and enjoyed retirement in the suburban borough of Old Meadow Lane, Hale in Altrincham, Cheshire. In late 2003, he relocated to a nursing home in the quiet leafy roads of Altrincham, passing away on 24 August 2004 due to a long battle with cancer. He was aged eighty-seven.

So if Pilkington was elsewhere during the Second World War, how could he appear in a document relating to W. E. Fairbairn? There only seem to be two realistic conclusions. One is that it was a different Mr William Pilkington completely. This is not totally implausible, but does seem rather unlikely. The other option is that the document itself is a forgery that has been passed off as being the genuine article for many a good year. The big lie is the one people believe, and the bigger the lie the more people will believe it. The anti-invasion document is the literal smoking gun, but who would have anything to gain by such a thing? Where did it originate from?

Pilkington started to raise a name for himself as a close quarter combat expert, who had studied under W. E. Fairbairn and E. A. Sykes, during the 1980s when he began to write for a number of survivalist and martial arts magazines on the subjects of close combat, self defence, and weapons tactics. He was well known among the army and military memorabilia fairs around the country. These articles with titles such as 'When a Weapon is Not a Weapon' appear to have brought him to the attention of Colonel Rex Applegate, a close combat instructor under Fairbairn during his time with the OSS in 1942. The two evidently found common ground, and Pilkington is known to have corresponded with

Applegate providing him with several pieces of research material that he claimed had come from his time working at the training camps in Scotland.

The anti-invasion document first appeared in print around the 1990s and is a source of reference in the book, *The Close Combat Files of Colonel Rex Applegate*, first published in 1998. The document was found among the files of the late Colonel Applegate following his death, and was included by the book's editor. People often quote from the Applegate book that Pilkington and Applegate actually met in the summer of 1942 when Applegate was seconded for a four-week training programme to the paramilitary camps in Scotland. As we now know, this could not have happened, as at the time, Bill Pilkington, as his military records show, was himself being 'reclassified as a Brakesman and Shunter—Class 3' on the trains as part of the 156 Trains Coy/Royal Engineers. This begs the question, was Applegate duped also? Pilkington was certainly well read on the whole SOE and commando subject matter, and had the ability to keep his answers 'vague.' It is certainly possible that he was able to blag his way through any questions that Applegate may have had for him.

Rex Applegate sadly passed away before the book was published, so we will never know for sure. We have to surmise that the editors of the book merely included the material that was found in Applegate's research documentation and assumed that Pilkington would have been at the special training centre where Applegate was being trained? It is certainly intriguing.

Who would gain in notoriety from this piece of material? Who was in contact with Rex Applegate during this period, and would often send him correspondence, who is mentioned in the document by name? William Pilkington. It returns to him. In intelligence circles it is known as the classic 'closed loop'. It is a piece of cast-iron information provided by, and mentioning the same person, and it was all given the stamp of approval by a recognised name of the close combat milieu.

I once heard the phrase; 'a secret agent is the one person in the world who will never tell you that he is a secret agent'. In William Pilkington's case the reverse seemed to be true—he could not wait to tell anyone who would listen that he had worked for British intelligence during the war—show business people, the press, secretaries. A whole host of people became aware of Pilkie's secret war, which, in itself, should speak volumes.

146

Throughout his postwar career he seemed to be modelling himself on that raconteur, David Niven, an actor who had had an interesting war with the commandos. He seemed to have a story for every occasion. It soon became apparent that the legendary twelve instructors, or at least the version that has been propagated by the likes of Pilkington and various researchers and subject matter experts, did not truly exist.

Let me clarify—I do believe that Fairbairn had a core of instructors working under him at various points in his career. Whether there was a cadre of twelve during July of 1940, is now open to doubt, and I suspect that for any researchers out there who wish to waste their time trying to find this close combat Eldorado, you may well be in for a very, very long hunt. I would further suggest that for any researchers and authors out there who had dealings with Mr Pilkington in the past, that you take any information he had regarding anything relating to his inside knowledge of Fairbairn and Sykes with a pinch of salt. Especially anything concerning Grant-Taylor, Sykes's personality, or the argument that is supposed to have happened between Fairbairn and Sykes during the time that Pilkington claims to have been working with them. I do not believe the twelve existed, and what is evident is that Bill Pilkington certainly was not one of them even if they did.

In the late 1980s, he had caught the eye of a new generation of combative students, and continued to promote himself as an instructor under Fairbairn. Indeed, one UK based combative group made a point of making him their group's patriarch, wholeheartedly believing his claims that there had been a direct lineage through Pilkington from Fairbairn to them. In addition to this, a wide range of self defence and combative instructors on both sides of the Atlantic, who were hoping to make a name for themselves, openly extolled about how they had trained with Pilkie, one of Fairbairn's protégés.

In the late 1990s, Pilkington offered to give a series of recorded interviews to the Imperial War Museum for posterity, relating his secret war experiences. This seems to have opened the floodgates as his name subsequently appeared in numerous books, articles, and TV shows, as a recognised authority on the whole SOE/Fairbairn industry. The tales grew and grew, with him having been, at various times, a commando, a bodyguard or an agent of British intelligence.

Pilkington fooled all of us for a very long time, including me up to a point. I wrote a short article about him in 2005-6. In it, I too fell for his mythology. Looking back it was a poorly written and researched piece that was hastily produced. I cringe every time I look at it for being so vague and a bit woolly. It was not well received, and to those I offended by it, I apologise.

When I went back to re-do the piece in detail several years later, and with more of an open mind to his accounts, it did not take long for me to realise that his story did not stack up. Not unless he had a teleportation device to whisk him from one part of the world to another at a moment's notice. The counter-argument usually presented at this point is that Pilkington could have been genuine and that perhaps it was all cover.

It is a nice, convenient, idea, but it is one that does not stand up to scrutiny when looked at forensically, and smacks of a lack of under-standing of how intelligence agents and operations were organised during the war. The first question that should be asked is, could Pilkington prove where he claimed he was during 1940-45? There would have been transfer files, orders, charges, travel papers, promotion requests. I suspect he could not, as most of his proof was anecdotal at best.

The second question should be, could the Army prove where he was and what units he belonged to? The answer to that would be yes, the military personnel file can prove where he was and in glorious detail. As for his military record being cover for his secret activities, well we need to keep things in perspective. When a serving soldier was transferred or attached to SOE or any of the special training schools it was noted in his Statement of Services file, a document that everyone involved in the military has. It would say that the soldier was to be 'specially employed' under one of the organisations cover names such as the Inter-Services Research Bureau or the Joint Technical Board. We have seen this, amongst others, with the Grant-Taylor investigation.

The military archives and personnel files are nothing if not accurate and detailed, with no stone left uncovered, and over the course of the research for this book I have reviewed many wartime SOE agents and military officers files to be easily able to recognise a transfer to be 'specially employed' by one of the numerous intelligence organisations. Once again we need to keep things in perspective regarding cover. At best, if we are to believe the story, Pilkington was an assistant instructor at one of the STS's. Whilst certainly different, it was by no means unique.

So creating this elaborate cover, consisting of falsifying his military files with a fake career path, for a mere junior instructor, would be stretching it a little, even for the people at SOE. Why bother when they could just request that he be detached to a cover organisation until further notice. Besides, during 1940-41, SOE had bigger issues with having to worry about actual cover identities for agents being flown into France, rather than worrying about a Lance-Corporal allegedly teaching up in the far outreaches of the Highlands of Scotland.

The argument of it all being cover, which can never truly be proved either way, is a breeding ground for people who like to immerse themselves in a certain type of mystique, like Pilkington. The 'hush, hush, wink, wink—can't talk about it, old boy' line is their get out of jail free card when they run short of stories, or they get dangerously close to being discovered. In short, hiding behind the argument of cover is the last refuge of the scoundrel. Our job as researchers and investigators is to simply deal with the historical, documented, and provable facts, nothing more. Anything else is just fiction.

Once again it was another in-depth investigation that took eighteen months to work through and to finally achieve a clear understanding of the facts. More disturbing was the serious repercussions from the testimonies about his past, and what was subsequently passed on through the people who idolised him. The damage he did with his falsehoods, hyperbole, myth, and innuendo is immeasurable. The blind faith of the people who revered him as a combatives hero has also done much to disrupt our understanding of the history of close quarter combat.

People may think it is easy to say this after the man is dead, and that the dead are a soft target. Perhaps, although people are quick to criticise picking on the deceased, it does not mean that he should not be exposed as a sham. There are many individuals over recent years who have gone to their graves seemingly as heroes, only for the public to latterly discover that they were anything but, in fact they were downright villains. Should we say nothing simply because they have passed on? I believe not. We owe it to future generations to get accurate information out there, and burying our heads in the sand seems very much like acquiescing and complying with the falsehood. If this information had been available whilst he was alive, I imagine that people would have had no qualms about confronting him with it, as many have done with a whole host of charlatan special forces heroes over the last twenty years.

Combative history experts and aficionados who have championed Pilkington, need to take a step back, reason out the facts for themselves and accept that they have had their illusions shattered and have been conned. This book is about reporting the factual truth, and not supporting the ramblings of a fantasy.

There will be people out there who will not want to believe the truth, and no matter how much evidence is presented, they will continue to believe the fable. They have invested too much time and effort in their chosen interpretation of history to back down and accept the truth without looking foolish. They are never going to be convinced, and in all honesty, this information, or perhaps even this book, is not written for them. It is written for people who have an interest in the correct factual history of Second World War close combat, and the people who shaped that type of training. I will let people make up their own minds about Pilkington and similar people, and say no more about it.

Over the years there have been many confusing and outlandish stories about the instructors and operators of those dark days of the Second World War. Some from pure inaccurate research, and some from downright untruths propagated by the personalities involved. Myths and legends have been created falsely and have, over time, gathered momentum and taken on distortions of the truth on an epic scale. Again, the big lie is the one that people will believe, and the bigger the lie the more people will believe it.

I believe what is needed now for students of close quarter combat history, is a moment of reflection and to take a pause. We were all duped to a certain degree, and the information we thought was genuine and accurate, from the horse's mouth, or so we thought, should be re-evaluated and picked apart. We should take nothing for granted. Check, check and check again should be the mantra. Believe nothing but the cold hard facts, *inquisitorem caveat*. Only then will we, as researchers, start the long road to find the truth about what went on, who the real personalities were during those dark days of the Second World War, and what we can learn for future generations of CQB students.

I hope that *At Close Quarters* has at least gone someway towards starting that journey.

Acknowledgements

No book is ever written in isolation. Certainly on this book there were a host of people that helped to contribute with information, assistance and general support.

Among those I would like to give a special nod to are the following people and contributors:

First and foremost, the family, for putting up with me during this project and for all your support. Love you all.

Joss O'Kelly and Keith O'Kelly, for an invaluable insight into Hector Grant-Taylor during his latter days in Quetta, and at the CQB School, and for all their support throughout this project. Without them this book would never have made it this far.

To the late Monty Hughes, for sharing his experiences of training in the Grant-Taylor pistol shooting method and of his time in Palestine, Burma and India.

The staff at the Imperial War Museum London, for making a stranger from the north feel very welcome on a freezing cold day in January many years ago.

Mary Pring at the FCO for helping me track down a certain lady.

The staff at the National Archives in Kew.

Roddy at the Military Records Office for all his assistance.

Andrew Dolan and Dorata Walker at the British Library, London.

Mark Seaman and the various members of the Special Forces Club, who made me welcome and helped me out with their time and wisdom.

Major Duncan at the Ministry of Defence, for all his help and positive comments about this book. An officer and a gentleman.

The staff at Wirral Archives, and at the Liverpool Reference Library.

Everyone at WW2Talk, especially Swiper, Psywar.org, Drew, and the Hebridean Chindit who came to the rescue at various times during the research. Old Bill thanks you.

Sue Farrington of the British Association of Cemeteries in South Asia (BACSA) for her help in tracking down G-T's final resting place, Sue was one of those people throughout this project that was always on hand with a contact or some inside knowledge. Thank you ma'am.

Geoff Murray and Jack Backer of the Commando Veterans Association (CVA) for allowing me to use their photos of Inverailort House.

Kirsten Hall and Liz Abbott for allowing me into their respective family histories.

US based Second World War Combatives researcher Dave Kentner for providing the initial information relating to the two articles written about Hector Grant-Taylor during the 1940s. Dave in many respects started the ball rolling, and I would urge anyone interested in accurate Second World War Combatives history to seek out his articles, material and counsel.

Captain John Bethell, Assistant Military Attaché in Pakistan for putting his contacts to work in the search for the Silver Lady and for his advice on travelling to Pakistan.

Marcia and the staff at Mount St Mary's College, Yorkshire for clearing up the confusion about Grant-Taylor's schooling.

Jane Keskar of The Kipling Society.

Those surviving former members of SOE and commando units that were happy to put me straight regarding any of my initial inaccuracies.

John Cameron, for sharing his fine collection of scenes from the Scottish Highlands.

The word *ka-tet* (on the dedication page) is taken from the Dark Tower series of books by Stephen King. The books deal with a quest, love, loss, life, death, kinship, rebirth and the art of the gunslinger, which in retrospect is more relevant to this tale of Grant-Taylor than I first thought.

Max Cooper, for allowing me to use his grandfather's account of Grant-Taylor during his time in Burma. For those wishing to see the original article it can be found at www.peterandmoiracooper.net

My friend and patron for this book, Lord (The Viscount) John Slim, member of the House of Lords and former Commanding Officer of 22 Special Air Service. Viscount Slim very kindly hosted me in London at the House of Lords and at the Special Forces Club on numerous occasions and was kind enough to offer valuable insight into his time training under Grant-Taylor, as well as the development of CQB that he instigated during his time with special forces. He, more than anyone, has helped push this project along, and I also owe him a debt of gratitude for writing the foreword to this book. Thank you Sir.

Those former, and still serving, members of special forces who were kind enough to put up with my damned impertinent questions. They have chosen to remain anonymous and I will honour that request.

For those of you wanting to have a more in-depth look at the life of Eric Anthony Sykes, SOE's infamous silent killing instructor, I recommend that you search out Marcus Binney's excellent, *Secret War Heroes: The Men of Special Operations Executive.*

Alan Sutton and Jasper Hadman at Fonthill Media for having faith in a new author. Thank you.

All my fellow investigators and operators from the network across the globe that helped me track down clues, leads and information in various countries.

The team from the Modern Combatives Group; Andy G, Dan M, Jamie H, Dave M, Mike B, but especially my good friend Dan Webster for sharing his knowledge over the years. These lads have showed loyal support and helped at every turn. We have over a decade or more trained hard, kept the faith, been bruised, battered and shed blood for the cause and we've also had a few laughs along the way. Lads you are gunslingers one and all.

And finally to a gentleman who is never mentioned in this book, for reasons of both operational and personal security, but who has been concealed in the shadows of this story and throughout these pages for many, many years. He is one those silent heroes who has been an inspiration and role model to me over the years in my CQB training, and without whom ... Thank you 'Alex'.

Bibliography

Applegate, Rex, *The Close Combat Files of Colonel Rex Applegate*, 1998, Paladin Press

Binney, Marcus, *Secret War Heroes: The Men of Special Operations Executive*, 2006, Hodder

Botting, Douglas, *Gavin Maxwell: A Life*, 1994, Harper Collins

Bracegirdle, Cyril, *Bill Pilkington Obituary*, 2004, *The Independent*

Broadhead, G. A. (With Hector Grant-Taylor), *Close Quarter Battle Manual/Palestine Police Force*, 1943, Government Printer, Palestine

Cesarani, David, *Major Farran's Hat: Murder, Scandal and Britain's Secret War Against Jewish Terrorism 1945–1948*, 2009, William Heinemann

Chaplin, H. D., *The Queen's Own Royal West Kent Regiment 1920-1950*, Naval & Military Press

Collins, Frank, *Baptism of Fire*, 1997, Doubleday

Connor, Ken, *Ghostforce: The Secret History of The SAS*, 2002, Cassell

Fairbairn, W. E., *Pistol Shooting*, 1927, The American Rifleman

Fairbairn, W. E., *Scientific Self Defense*, 1931, D. Appleton & Co.

Fairbairn, W. E. (with E. A. Sykes), *Shooting To Live*, 1942, Oliver And Boyd

Fairbairn, W. E., *All-In Fighting*, 1942, Faber & Faber

Farran, Roy, *Winged Dagger: Adventures on Special Service*, 1998, Cassell

Ford, Roger (With Tim Ripley), *The Whites of Their Eyes*, 1997, Sidgwick & Jackson

Geraghty, Tony, *The Bullet-Catchers*, 1989, Grafton Books

Geraghty, Tony, *Who Dares Wins: The Story Of The SAS*, 2002, Abacus

Hall, R. F., *Personal Memories of F&S*, 2005, BBC WW2 Peoples War Website

Hilsman, Roger, *American Guerilla: My War Behind Japanese Lines*, 1990, Brassey's

Kent, Ron, *First In: Parachute Pathfinder Company*, 1979, Harper Collins

King, Stephen, *The Dark Tower: Wizard And Glass*, 2003, Hodder

Laville, Sandra, 'Keepers of Britsih War Graves Pay The Price', 2001, *The Daily Telegraph*

Mcgivern, Ed, *Fast and Fancy Revolver Shooting*, 1975, Winchester Press

Ranfurly, Countess of, *To War With Whitaker*, 1997, Mandarin

Robins, Peter, *Gentleman & Warrior: The Legend of W. E. Fairbairn*, 2009, CQB Publications

Scholey, Pete, *The Joker*, 2007, Andre Deutsch Ltd

Scholey, Pete, *SAS Heroes*, 2008, Osprey

Sondern Jnr, Frederick, *Murder is His Business*, 1943

Thompson, Julian, *Forgotten Voices of Burma: The Second World War's Forgotten Conflict*, 2010, Ebury Press

Tinney, Cal, *Hectors Job Was Murder*, 1949, Fawcett Publications Ltd

West, Nigel, *Secret War: The Story of SOE*, 1992, Hodder & Stoughton

Wilkinson, Peter (with Joan Bright Astley), *Gubbins & SOE*, 1993, Pen & Sword

Ziegler, Philip, *Personal Diary of Admiral The Lord Louis Mountbatten, Supreme Allied Commander 1943–46*, 1988, Collins

Index

Grant-Taylor, Sophie, 46, 97, 98,
Grenzschutzgruppe 9, 122,
GSG-9, 122,
Gubbins, Major Colin McVeigh,
  34, 35, 141, 155,
HM Wormwood Scrubs, 28, 29,
Hall, Major R. F. 'Henry', 43, 44,
  155,
Heckler and Koch 9-mm MP5
  sub-machine gun, 121,
Hickok, Wild Bill, 55, 92,
Hicks, William, 97, 98, 111,
Hilsman, Major Roger 'Tex', 92,
  155,
Howrah Train Station, Calcutta,
  89,
Independent Companies, 34, 35,
Ingram M10 sub-machine gun,
  121,
Inns of Court Officer Training
  Centre, 19,
Inter-Service Research Bureau,
  34,
Inverailort House, 35, 43, 49,
  152,
Iranian Embassy, 123,
Irgun, 114,
Irregular Warfare Training
  Centre, 35,
Jennings, Colonel, 73,
Joint Technical Board, 34, 148,
Keeni-Meeni, 119,
Kenya, 117,
Khan, Ayub, 108,
Khan, Sultan Mohammed, 105,
Killing House, 104, 115, 117,
  121, 136,
CQB Building, 67, 121,

King David Hotel, 75, 114, 142,
King of Greece, George II of the
  Hellenes, 85,
Kipling, Rudyard, 15, 109, 152,
Kramer, Josef, 142,
Laborde, Kathleen Melita, 105,
  106,
Laborde, Mary, 109,
Lauder, Brigadier Ian, 102, 110,
Liverpool, 36, 37, 42, 47, 54, 109,
  141, 142, 144, 145, 152,
Lochailort, 35, 43, 49, 50,
Long Range Desert Group, 82,
LRDG, 82,
Luftwaffe, 13, 78, 79, 80, 131,
Macgregor, Alastair, 115,
Malay Scouts, 116, 117,
Maxwell, Gavin, 51, 154,
Maxwell, Terence, 53,
Mayne, Major Robert Blair
  (Paddy), 82,
McCann, Danny, 125, 126,
McConnell, Major-General D. F.,
  78,
Melewski, Mariam, 144,
Military Intelligence (Research),
  34,
MI(R), 35,
Mount Carmel, 66,
Mount St Mary's, 12, 16, 152,
Mountbatten, Lord Louis, 87, 94,
  97, 155,
Munro, General Sir Charles, 21,
Mystery Shoots, 64, 121,
Nanyuki, 117,
Nasik, 7, 94, 95,
Neuve Chappelle, 17,
New York Police Department, 61,

Small Scale Raiding Force (SSRF), 79,
Sondern Jnr, Frederick, 77, 78, 89, 155,
South East Asia Command (SEAC), 87, 94,
Special Air Service (SAS), 7, 80, 81, 116, 153,
Special Boat Section (SBS), 82,
Special Operations Executive (SOE), 11, 13, 16, 33, 34, 35, 43, 44, 48, 49, 50, 51, 52, 53, 58, 59, 65, 67, 68, 75, 76, 79, 80, 81, 89, 96, 113, 115, 122, 134, 140, 141, 142, 145, 146, 147, 148, 149, 152, 153,
Special Raiding Squadron (SRS), 82,
Special Training School (STS), 43, 48, 50, 51, 53, 58, 66, 68, 148,
Spin Baldak, 21,
Sterling, David, 43, 82,
Stern Gang, 114, 115,
STS 102, 53, 67, 68,
Sykes, Eric Anthony, 8, 9, 36, 37, 38, 39, 40, 41, 42, 43, 44, 45, 52, 57, 58, 59, 61, 62, 65, 73, 74, 83, 89, 104, 116, 121, 129, 133, 134, 141, 143, 145, 147, 153

Taylor Marsh, J. L., 22,
Taylor, Cyril, 16,
Taylor, Jane, 15, 17,
Taylor, John Henry, 15,
Taylor, Leonard, 15, 17, 18, 21, 22, 23, 24, 25, 133,
Terrell, Courtney, 19,
Third Afghan War, 21,
Thomas, Eleanor Ann, 27, 28,
Thompson Sub-Machine Gun, 65, 69,
Tommy Gun, 7, 65, 76, 78, 84, 88,
Tinney, Cal, 89, 155,
Tunbridge Wells, 18, 20, 49,
Twohig, Lt-Col. J. P. O'Brian, 43,
United States Marine Corps (USMC), 40, 89,
Wapshore, General Richard, 21,
Wavell, General Sir Archibald, 52, 53, 87,
Wilkinson, General Montague Grant, 20, 48, 49,
Williams, David, 83,
Wingate, Brigadier Orde, 69, 87, 115,
Winstead, Charles, 92,
Woodhouse, Arthur, 60,